How To Avoid

"Just Looking"

And Other Ways To Increase Your Retail Sales

by
Terry Kennon

Table of Contents

Introduction: About the Author and the Book

PART ONE: Setting the Stage

PART TWO: The Six Sales Steps

PART THREE: Specific Situations

Thanks to Brian, Maureen, Jacob, Reilly and Garrett. This book would not be here if not for them.

Introduction
About The Author and the Book

A wise old used car salesman named Bill once told me that the first thing to look for in any how-to-sell book was what experience the author had in sales. That would give you some idea if he had anything worth saying. As you know, a lot of sales books aren't very relevant. That's your first lesson from this book.

I got my sales experience by selling oak furniture as a street vendor in Washington D.C. from 1977 to 1982. I was taught by a former psychological operations officer from the Vietnam War. He had been thoroughly trained in all the aspects of the human psyche and how to guide it. Human behavior was definitely no mystery to him. It was fascinating using the different techniques he had learned. But in this book we are going to focus only on what you need to know to make a retail sale.

It's a long story but after the war ended in 1975, the psy-ops officer and I found ourselves raising four Vietnamese orphans on a small farm outside of Washington D.C. in Virginia. Out of necessity and fate we started the furniture business a couple of years later. Unable to afford a store, we took orders off of samples on the street corners in Washington between 11 a.m. and 3 p.m., lunch time. People would pick up their orders in our barn in Virginia.

Selling furniture on the street corner is much harder to do than in a store. You have no credibility, as street vendors have an unsavory reputation for shoddy goods and questionable business practices. The customers are going to lunch; they aren't looking for furniture at that time. And they are usually working so they don't have their spouse with them. With all of these negatives, I would still average three to five tables and two to four rocking chairs per four-hour day.

We opened our first store in 1979. In 1982 the store kept me too busy to sell on the street anymore. By 1989 we had grown to five stores in three states. Over the years I have trained many salespeople and managers in the art of sales. Through study and trial and error I have found what works best both in selling and in teaching selling.

Using the same techniques in the store that I had used on the street proved incredibly effective. I had the credibility of the store, the customers had their spouses and they were interested in buying furniture. It was like running with lead shoes and then taking them off. If you could sell furniture well on the street, you could sell it extremely well in a store!

Our competitors and suppliers were amazed at how much volume we did with minimal advertising. You don't need to advertise as much if you sell most of the people that walk through your door. And when they are sold correctly, the customers are more than happy to give you both repeat business and referrals.

So that's my experience with retail sales. I've done it long enough to say with confidence the techniques covered in this book work - and work incredibly well!

You can learn something new off of any page. As you can tell from the table of contents, this book covers all aspects of how to make a retail sale. The six steps are the part of the book you'll use every day. Keep them posted in your lunchroom. Follow these steps, complete each one in order and you'll do fine.

However, before I help you learn how to sell the customer; I'll start with what the customer thinks; the differences between men, women and couples; and how to set up a floor that's conducive to sales. Once you know this and have your stage set, it's time to sell!

PART ONE

SETTING THE STAGE

Chapter One
The Customer

You've opened a store. You've advertised. You've got the product. Now it's your job to sell the customers that come in. The first thing you need to know is who these people usually are and how they usually think. Notice I said "usually." When you're dealing with people, nothing is one hundred percent. You can predict what the masses will do, but there's always a Charles Manson, Gandhi, or Einstein in the bunch. Sales is about going with the odds. Go with the approach that works nine out of ten times, not one out of ten.

People are not machines. They have feelings, emotions, prejudices, memories, not to mention six senses. These factors must be taken into account when you're trying to sell a person. To ignore them is disastrous. So far in retail selling, most salespeople and managers ignore them, and treat people as though they were logical. If you deal with these human traits, your business will stand out in the customer's mind as a great place, and you'll have customer loyalty that's truly amazing. Just treat them like human beings. Simple!

When people go to shop for a big-ticket item, it's usually stressful for them. They need the item, but they are insecure about their ability to make the right decision. In their daily life they usually don't need to know that much about furniture, cars, etc. So they are venturing into unknown territory. They are worried about what their friends will think of their purchase. They're worried about making a wrong decision and wasting all that money.

It's your job to relieve them of this misery. One of the worst feelings in the world is being on "the horns of a dilemma", or not knowing which way to go. It drains a lot of energy from people and causes a lot of anxious moments. Once a decision has been made, you can see the relief come over the customers' faces. Now they can spend their weekends doing something they like instead of going to different furniture stores agonizing over a decision. And they get to enjoy their purchase! The cruelest thing you can do is not sell them and prolong this misery.

Don't worry about making the customers do something they don't want to do. It can't be done. I've tried. If it could be done, every home in Washington D.C. would have at least ten of our tables! Plus, governments and businesses all over the world would want to know the technique! It's the same rule as in hypnotism. You cannot make a person do something they really don't want to do. So give each customer your best shot. It's the nicest thing you can do for them. The customers that were the hardest to sell always thanked me at the end profusely. I was the only salesperson who stayed with them long enough to get them off of "the horns of a dilemma."

When most people go out to buy a table and chairs, they usually intend to do it like this: They plan to shop at different stores, comparing prices, styles, and quality. They will then take this information home and make a rational decision.

But people aren't logical like a computer. Hence they usually don't buy logically. Even though the above method is the best way to buy something, and most people set out to do it that way, they usually end up buying where they get caught up in the heat of desire created by the salesperson.

Most customers assume that the sales people they are going to talk to do not really know much about their product. They also assume that the salesperson is only concerned with making a sale so he can get a commission, not about their well being. Hence they don't want the salesperson around.

What they want in a salesperson is someone who is an expert about the product and whose advice can be trusted. Once you build up trust and convince them that you are there to help them make a good decision and not to get a commission out of them, they'll take your advice-which should be to buy your product.

Once you know what most customers are thinking and feeling; you are ready to meet this challenge in a way that makes for happy, satisfied customers!

Chapter Two

Shopping Traits of Men, Women, and Couples

Men, women and couples all act differently and need to be treated as such. Anytime you deal with people, nothing is going to happen one hundred per cent of the time, but a lot of things happen ninety per cent or more. I'm going to focus on what happens the vast majority of the time. That way you'll be right the vast majority of the time and wrong every once in a while. That seems a lot better than the other way around.

Men usually hate to shop. If a man needs an item, he will go directly to where it is. He usually buys the first thing someone sells him on that will do the job. Then, he's out of there.

On the other hand, a woman will usually shop all the stores she can. When she goes into a store, she'll look at what she needs, then look at everything else the store has.

The theory that makes the most sense in explaining this behavior is the hunter-gatherer theory. People were designed to live in small hunter-gatherer tribes. The men would go out in small groups and quietly look around for something that moved. Since there's not a lot of time to really study it before it runs or flies away, they would kill it as soon as they could. Then they would decide if it was a good thing. This seems to explain why they don't talk that much about anything and buy the first thing they see that they need.

Women would go out in large groups through fields of berries, etc. They would talk and gossip and study each plant for ripe fruit. If you picture the woman in a field gathering fruit the next time you watch her browse down an aisle, you'll be amazed at the similarity of her actions. This would seem to explain why most women seem to like to shop and are more patient about it. Most men don't like to shop and are not very patient about it. Remember, most means most, not all. There are always exceptions. Always bet with the odds.

In heterosexual couples, the woman is the one who usually makes the decision. This is especially true in furniture. It boils down to who cares the most about what you're selling. I think in almost all incidences, it is the woman who cares the most.

Think about it. If you sell the guy and not the woman, he'll ask her," What do you want to do?" She'll say, "Let's think about it." He'll say, "Okay." But if you sell the woman and not the guy, she'll ask, "What do you want to do?" He'll say, "Let's think about it." She'll ask, "Why?" Then she will proceed to sell him in ways you can't. Just shut up and let her go on it. Most times, at the critical point when he agrees with her you can come back and close them again and this time they will buy. I wondered for years why this was so. I have come to the conclusion that guys don't care about it as much. So in a war of attrition, the person who cares the most will win. Usually that person is the woman.

We had a couple in one time where the husband was a cabinetmaker. Once he realized all our products were made well, he told his wife to get whatever chair she wanted. He knew that was going to happen anyway, so why fight it? He went out in the parking lot to drink beer. She was trying to get his opinion on which of two chairs to get. He came in, saw the two and said, "Whichever one you want is fine with me." She said for him to sit in them and see which one was best. He sat in both and said, "They're both fine." She asked, "Which one do you like?" He said, "They're both great! They keep my ass off the floor. They do everything I want a chair to do!" The point is the man usually doesn't take the purchase of furniture as seriously as the woman does. Usually his main concern is the price of the purchase. His preference is the cheapest way to do the job. But if her preference is a different item, she's probably the one that won't give. So sell her. When mom is happy, everybody is happy. When mom isn't happy, it's a bad scene.

I have seen guys who say they have to bring their wife back. They say they bought a table without her approval twenty years ago, and they haven't heard the end of it yet. She's constantly pointing out what's wrong with it. They'll never do that again. It's not worth it.

Be polite to the guy, but sell the woman. If they split up and look around the store separately for a while, stick with the woman. She's the one you have to sell.

The ones with the power are usually quiet and secure in the knowledge that they will be the ones that make the ultimate decision. This makes them more serious. The ones without the power will be more relaxed. A rule of thumb is the louder they are, the less power they have. So don't be fooled. It's the quiet ones you have to watch. This is why you direct your initial greeting to the guy. He's more relaxed and will usually tell you what he's looking for. The woman will probably tell you they are just looking. She knows she's the one making the decision and doesn't want to be led astray by a salesperson. She wants to decide on her own. This is why as soon as you find out what they are looking for, you direct your questions to the woman.

If the guy is trying to take control, try to get it back to where the woman is doing most of the talking. I've seen situations where the husband is listing off everything they are going to buy while the wife is letting him. Then, at the last moment, the wife says something that nixes the whole deal, and they leave. Letting the man take control of the situation is usually a waste of time.

A lot of times the guy doesn't know that the woman is calling the shots. I've seen guys say, "We're getting this chair and that's it!" Then he walks off. I've seen the wife then say to the woman salesperson, "Don't worry, I'll handle him." And twenty minutes later he's saying he changed his mind, he's going to get what she wanted. But it's done in such a way that he still thinks he called that one. Meanwhile, the whole sales staff is laughing at him behind his back and the wife is smiling knowingly, and he has no clue what's really going on. It's embarrassing to be a guy sometimes.

I saw one husband handle it with good humor. He said, "I have a house; when she's not there. I have two cars; when she doesn't need them. I have two horses; when she doesn't want to ride them." His wife then said,

"Hey, what do I always tell you?" They then both said in unison, "You the man!"

One time we had a guy come in to buy a table. The salesman was the old used car salesman I mentioned in the beginning of the book. He asked the customer if his wife needed to see it first, and the guy said, "No, I buy all the stuff that goes into the house." The salesman said, "And there's no problem?" The man said no, and the salesman said, "Really? This is the first time I've seen this. Can I have your autograph?" The customer started to get uncomfortable, so I had to step in and write the order before the old guy blew the sale. That's how rare that is. Most guys think it's an equal decision, but it's not. And they really don't care that much anyway.

We heard a down-home country car mechanic explain it this way. A couple left in a huff because he wanted one thing and she wanted another. He saw it happen and said, "She'll just cut him off from sex. Tomorrow he'll be calling begging to have what she wants delivered now!" That's another theory. Who knows why it's true, it just is!

So be polite to the guy, but sell the wife. In same sex couples, you have to figure out from observation which one is running the show and sell that one. Look for the quiet one, the one the other one asks questions to. The one the other one follows is the person to sell.

If you've been selling any length of time and think back, you know what I say is true. Don't judge people, just treat them as they are, not as you want them to be.

Chapter Three

Preparing Your Sales Floor

Or Setting the Stage

The first thing you want to do is set up your floor so that people feel comfortable making a decision to buy your product. Setting up your floor to make it easier to sell is something you can control. In sales there are enough things out of your control, so you don't need to add to them. Things out of your control during a sale include babies starting to cry or worse, kids running amok, loud obnoxious customers in the background, having to answer a ringing phone... and the list goes on and on. All of these things and more have broken the flow of a sale and blown it. And there was nothing that could be done to prevent them from happening. The things you can control, control them! If you notice something wrong, fix it immediately.

When people come into a store, they have a tendency to flow to the right. You'll notice that grocery and other stores are set up so when you come in you have no choice but to go right. Try to have your store flow to the right and put the stuff you want to push to the right. If someone comes in and goes to the left, then you know they've probably been in before and came back to see something you have on the left side. People just don't normally come in a place for the first time and turn left.

It's good to keep your low to mid-price merchandise up front. The expensive items usually look the best, and a lot of sales people want to put the best-looking items up front. People who can't afford it see the prices and figure everything in the store is this price range, so they walk out. Or they see the best right away and nothing else measures up, including their finances. People who can afford anything in the store will see good quality mid-price merchandise in front and walk through the store, and so will people who have a limited budget.

People have six senses. Take each one into consideration when you set up your floor. I'll start with the sense of Sight. Your floor should be set up so that it's pleasing to the eye and organized so it looks like you know what you're doing. This builds confidence in your customers. All the sets should blend in well. There should be no obvious flaws in the product. In furniture, all the boards should blend in well.

Smart people assume your samples are your best pieces. If your samples don't look so nice, they assume this is as good as it gets.

If one customer tells you that he sees something wrong with a sample, rest assured that hundreds more saw it. They just didn't tell you. This can result in hundreds of lost sales if you don't correct it. So fix it as soon as possible. To lose a sale because of something you saw before but didn't fix is just not good sense.

When I was selling on the street corners the samples had to be more than perfect. I had a lot of unusual obstacles to contend with. People were very suspicious of the quality. One day I noticed my table had a glue seam showing on one of the legs. I'd had people object to these before. The raised seams made people suspicious that the furniture would crack once you got it home, with no one to take it back to. They figured that was one reason why it was so cheap. Fortunately for me no one seemed to notice, but my sales that day were down. That night I switched legs. The next day a man came up with a woman and said to her, "That's the table I was telling you about. But he has a different table today; the one yesterday had a glue seam in the leg". That's how I realized that if they see something wrong with the sample, they usually won't say anything to you about it, they just won't buy it. Then you get confused as to why no one is buying.

The customers are already insecure about buying anything. They're afraid they will get the wrong thing for their needs, pay too much for it, or get ridiculed by their friends about their purchase. So there's no reason to make it easier for them to rationalize not buying. You can explain to them why their concerns about the sample are no problem, but usually once the doubt is there, it stays. So avoid these situations.

I only had one customer who understood the rationale behind picking the sample. I would take orders on the street. It was my job to convince the customer he was better off giving me a refundable deposit for an order than just getting my card. The customers would come out to a barn to pick up their order. One guy insisted on buying the sample outright. It had taken me hours to pick out a "perfect sample." I tried to talk him in to picking up a nice new one. He said, "Why? I know this is the best looking one you have, it's your sample." So that night I spent hours picking out another sample. He knew!

Another important part to setting up your floor is price tags, Make sure everything that needs a tag has one. If you have to go look up a price on an item because the price tag is missing, not only does it break the flow of the sale but also it makes you look incompetent. You want to give them the confidence they need to give you their money.

It is good to make your price tags easy to read. If the customers see an item and exclaim how much they like it, then see the price is higher than they can afford, they probably won't buy anything. There are two reasons for this. One, nothing lower priced will probably be as nice, so that will frustrate them. Two, the main reason it will mess up the sale is that customers will probably be embarrassed to admit they can't afford it. To save face they will either find something wrong with it or say they have to go home and measure or something else like that. They usually really hate to say they can't afford it so they will come up with a different excuse. The best way to handle any problem is to avoid it if possible. If your prices are easy to see, then he automatically knows he can't afford it and discounts it from consideration.

Never have two items next to each other that make it difficult for the customer to decide, like a really nice expensive model setting next to a less nice, cheaper version of the same thing. That makes it hard for people who can only afford the cheaper one to buy it. They can compare it to a nice one right there, but can't afford it.

Now they won't be satisfied with the cheaper one and have to go home and think about it.

Keep all similar items with similar prices together so you don't have to run all over the store to show them. You'll lose the flow of the sale. Do whatever you can do to make it easier for you. It's hard enough to narrow the customer's choice down to one item!

It's been proven in studies that the best colors for a sign or price tag are a yellow background with black letters. The second best combination is a red background with white letters. These color combinations stand out without being offensive to most people. Day glo orange stands out, but most people aren't going to be comfortable with it. This is why school buses and stop signs are the color they are as well as Cheerios and Coca-Cola. The next time you go to a grocery store, notice all the yellow and black, red and white packaging on the shelves. There's a reason.

The other proven color is gray. Things stand out better on a gray background. So having your furniture on a gray floor or carpet is a good thing. The shapes and colors are more defined. Notice the next time the trees and landscape stand out much better against a gray sky. You'll see what I mean.

The sales floor is your stage, with your role being the knowledgeable professional. Your dress and appearance is important. You should try to blend in with your surroundings so that the attention is on the furniture, not on you. On the street I would wear nice casual clothes while talking to customers in suits. They felt comfortable with me. Had I worn the usual street vendor dress of blue jeans and tee shirt or a suit and tie like the customers, they would have felt uncomfortable with me.

When I was in the barn, I would change into blue jeans. I didn't stand out in their mind, the furniture did. You will have to be the judge of what is appropriate dress at your store. It's trial and error. If you have success dressing a certain way, keep doing it. If you have a series of bad days, try another look. That's the only way to find out. But when you are trying to decide what's best, take into consideration your surroundings, knowing you want to blend in. If it's an upscale retail place, dress upscale. In a warehouse-store operation, dress down. It's all trial and error. Blue and green clothing seemed to have a calming effect on people in the store.

I had a lucky shirt that I would wear when I really needed to do well. My psychological operations officer friend took a color class. My shirt was rust colored, and he knew it had always been my lucky shirt. He said the teacher told him rust drew attention and made people do impulsive things. It was weird because I always did well on the street with that shirt. So he went out and bought six rust colored shirts. But they were a different shade of rust from my original shirt and didn't seem to work as well.

Later I saw on a TV news show that a study found the color pink physically weakened men. They did an experiment where a group of men lifted a certain weight dumbbell with no problem. Then they put a large pink colored poster in front of their face, and the men had trouble lifting the same weight they had no problem with earlier. A warden in a small town somewhere saw this and decided to paint his drunk tank pink to weaken the drunken rages in there. The first time he tried it out, the drunks tore the place apart. This color pink enraged them. So he checked with the people who did the study and found out he had used the wrong shade of pink. So it's not only the color, it has to be the right shade of that color to get the desired effect.

Oh, by the way, once my friend found out about rust, he painted the outside of all of our stores rust! Attract attention and make people do impulsive things. Every little bit helps! People are affected by all kinds of things, including color.

The sense of Smell is important to selling. Everyone knows that baking apple pies while showing your house to potential buyers will make it easier to sell. We used to polish the furniture with Guardsman cream polish, and people would comment that they liked our store because it smelled like wood. It didn't smell like wood, it smelled like Guardsman, but we kept polishing with it for that reason. The department store Nordstrom's is a good example of the total stage for retail. They have their own special scent wafting through the store to make it more pleasant and conducive to buying for their customers.

The sense of Touch is also important to selling. The more people touch the product, the more they want it. They'll follow your cue. If you touch the furniture lovingly and with respect, they usually will too. It's the monkey see, monkey do thing. Some of my salespeople had sold insurance before working for me. They said one reason selling furniture was easier was because the customer could see it and feel it. Selling an idea or concept like insurance was much harder to do. Needless to say, the insurance guys sold a lot of furniture!

The sense of Hearing is really important. You usually want it quiet enough so customers can hear you and not be distracted. Any non-stop music or noise will eventually win over people's attention. It just doesn't stop. Ever. TV and radio abhor dead air. In normal human conversation there are pauses. That's when the radio or TV takes over and never lets go. So if you're going to sell someone you must have their undivided attention and they must have yours.

We rented part of another furniture store's floor once. We sold our furniture and theirs. It had Muzak piped in. Muzak is great in a grocery or other stores where the customer is on their own. It relaxes their mind. It's not good if you are trying to personally sell them. After a few hours of listening to muzak, my mind was total mush. I couldn't think straight, let alone try to sell someone. No way. After a few weeks, I finally convinced them to turn it off. They hadn't noticed because they never tried to actually sell anyone in that store. They basically just waited for someone to give them an order. Their sales increased noticeably once we pulled the plug.

While driving downtown to sell on the street, I would repeat my table presentation out loud until I said it without a mistake. Then I'd listen to the radio. Ten minutes before I got to the corner, I would turn it off. This helped me get focused on selling the furniture. If I was listening to the radio all the way there, my concentration and focus would not be there. In sales you have to be focused and in the moment.

After spending day after day in the store, salespeople tend to forget they are in a public place. It starts to feel like a second home and the customers blend in with the scenery. This is dangerous. I've heard salespeople say, "Who's up?" or "You take him" loud enough for all the customers in the store to hear when a new customer walks in! They totally forget the customer can hear them. I've seen them gossip about customers in front of other customers, complain about working conditions, chat about what they did last night, etc. It's very embarrassing to watch. Such sales people are oblivious to the customer. This is not good if your purpose is to try and sell as many customers as you can. It makes the customer feel like an unimportant piece of meat. It's a very insulting thing to do to another human being. Unless they really, really want something, they won't buy.

It's easy to start seeing the store as a second home. Salespeople have to be reminded from time to time that they're in a public place. If you watch the whole scene while it happens, you become embarrassed for the sales person. It really makes them look bad. Remember, on this stage the real star of the show is the customer, not you.

That's another common mistake by salespeople. Everyone usually prefers to talk about themselves, sales people and customers alike. Remember, the customers are writing the checks. Let them talk about themselves. Your job is to steer it to a sale. That's all. When customers have a pleasant buying experience, they will come back for more stuff later if they need it and refer their friends to you.

Of course the way you speak is very important when you consider the sense of hearing. Music and hypnotism can lull people into various stages of powerful trances. It's a powerful sense. You want to speak clearly and not in a monotone. Raise and lower your voice in a rhythmic way to both hold the customer's attention and lull him into a trance like state. Also if you naturally move your hands while you talk, that's even better. It holds the customers' attention. A good salesperson really almost hypnotizes the customer.

The sense of Taste never came into play in retailing furniture at our store. The only thing we would offer would be ice water on the really hot days to make customers more comfortable and less irritable. If you do have food or coffee in your operation, make sure it tastes good! Common sense!

The sixth sense plays a big role in selling. In our culture there's not an official name for this intuitive sense that I know of. A friend and I were having lunch with a woman from Indonesia. He asked her what they thought of Extra Sensory Perception in Indonesia. She said, "Well, there we don't call it extra." That was a good answer, I thought.

You can tell by the feel in air if someone is angry, happy, or sad. You can feel if someone is looking at you or if they're behind you. The customer can, too. That is why you want pleasant feelings in your store. It creates a great atmosphere. We kept a Far Side daily calendar on the counter for customers to read while their order was being written. It helped lighten their mood. A happy cheery place is very important. Try to keep all bad feelings away from the stage. Disney World has a huge sign above the exit of the employee dressing room. It says SMILE. Smiling is contagious.

The bottom line is people are mirrors of you. If you're happy, confident and genuinely interested in your product, the customer will be too. If you're not, the customer will have to want it real bad to buy it from you. Take these facts about human beings and accept and deal with them. Your sales will go up, the customer will be happier and so will you!

Now you have an idea of how the customers behave and how to set up a comfortable environment for them to make a decision to buy.

PART TWO

THE
SIX STEPS

Chapter Four

The Six Steps of A Retail Sale

Now we are getting into the meat of the book: how to continually make sales in such a way that you insure customer loyalty and satisfaction. There are six basic steps needed to make a retail sale. They must be successfully completed one at a time in order to make a retail sale. Since it's not door-to-door sales, the customer that walks into your store usually has some interest in what you have or they wouldn't be there. Advertising or signs do the door-to-door sales step of getting their attention and interest. The following are the six steps of a retail sale.

Step One: The Greeting.
Step Two: The Presentation.
Step Three: How Long Has the Customer Been Looking?
Step Four: What Exactly Does the Customer Want?
Step Five: When Does the Customer Want It?
Step Six: Close the Sale.

The purpose of the greeting is to find out what in general the customer is looking for while avoiding the dreaded "just looking" response. Once you know what they want, the presentation is designed to build up their desire for your product. It also makes customers more forthright in their answers to your questions. Asking how long they have been looking for this item lets you know whom you're dealing with. If they've been looking a while, then they'll know what you have is a good deal. If they just started looking and yours is the first place they've looked, they may not be as sure. Finding out exactly what they want is when you narrow down their choices on a particular item to the one that best suits them. You can't ask customers to buy something unless you know exactly what they want to buy. Once you know what they want, then you need to know when they want it. That way you can tailor your close to their needs. You'll know whether to close them on something in stock or close for a future order, without finding out after the close that they wanted it now or later. Once you know what they want, when they want it, and have built up a desire for that item, then you close the sale and ask them to buy it.

These steps have to be done in order. You can't skip around. First, you have to find out what the customers want. Otherwise you don't know which item to sell them. Next, build up their desire for your line, otherwise you'll get guarded vague answers to your questions and they won't be interested enough to buy anything. Now that they are giving you straighter answers, ask how long they've been looking, so you know how much knowledge they have about other stores and the item. Finding out exactly what they want lets you know what you're asking them to buy. You can't ask when they want it until you know what they want. Asking when they want it gives you the final piece of the whole picture. Following these steps in order, you'll now know what they want, you'll know when they want it, and by this time you will have stoked the fires of desire for it. So now you close them with a tailor-made close.

Completing each step in order is the only way to go. Now we'll look at each step in detail.

Chapter Five

Step One: The Greeting

The purpose of the greeting is to find out what the customers are looking for and to take control of the situation. You can't sell them something until you're in control and you know what they want. If you're not in control and don't know what they want, you're in a passive position, and the only thing you can do is take an order if you're lucky enough for the customer to give you one. You'll have many more sales if you perfect a greeting.

Remember that all the customers know is that they are going to walk in to the store. Some salesperson is going to walk up to them and ask, "May I help you?" They are going to say, "Just looking." The salesperson is going to say, "Oh, okay. If you have any questions, let me know." That's all they know. If you can get around this situation, they are in uncharted territory. They have no idea what is going to happen next. If you're confident and friendly, they'll follow you anywhere.

And you should be able to get around it. The odds are in your favor. You know what to say. You know where everything is in the store. You've been doing it long enough you know where the customers usually stop, what they usually ask, etc. The customers don't stand a chance!

When I sold on the street corner, I noticed how much it was like fishing. You put out your bait - your merchandise and signs - at a good spot, which was the corner. The people would school by and then would stop and nibble on the bait. If I greeted them too fast or too strong, it would scare them off. I had yanked the bait right out of their mouths. If I waited too long to greet them, they would study the sample long enough and then ask for a business card. In other words, they would run off with the bait. Timing is everything on the greeting. You can't be too fast or too slow, too rough or too meek. You can't reel them in until you hook them.

What you want to do is find a greeting system that works most of the time. Nothing involving people will work 100% of the time, but you can find things that will work 90% of the time. By the time the greeting is over you should know what your customers are looking for. You can then put yourself in control and lead them to the item they need so you can give them a presentation on it. The greeting is a subtle power play that determines who is going to take control. If you take control, you will probably have a sale. If the customers take control, they will probably go home to think about it. You don't want that! The customers will give you control and tell you what they want if they feel comfortable with you. To get them comfortable, there are four things to take into consideration: what words to say, how to say them, where to stand when the customer comes in, and how to stand. All four of these are important. The greeting example I'm going to give you will work in just about any retail setting. But remember they are not magic words. They will only work if you say them in the right way at the right time and place.

ONE
What to Say and Why

I've found that any number of greetings will work. We had one salesperson who would start out talking about the weather, the customer's kids, what someone was wearing, it all depended on the customer that came in. Then she would ask them what they were looking for after the initial small talk got them comfortable with her. This works. But she was under constant stress because she never knew exactly what she was going to say until the customer came in and she sized them up. I found it much more relaxing to say the same thing each time, knowing it will work most of the time. It freed my mind to concentrate on the customer. Her mind was on what she was going to say to the next people in the door.

We started out using various greetings in different stores, such as "What brings you in today" and "What were you mostly interested in?" It depended on the store and the salesperson. They all worked. We eventually evolved to the "Yes, sir?" greeting which worked in all of our stores, and all of the salespeople felt comfortable saying it. It goes like this:

"Hi!" (Say as soon as the customer comes through the door.)

"Yes, sir?" (Say this while the customer has stopped for the first time.)

"Just looking."

"Oh, Okay. What were you looking for?"

"Tables."

"Is it for a dining room or kitchen?"

"Kitchen."

"Oh, okay. Which wood do you prefer?"

"Oak."

"They're this way. " (Start walking toward tables.) "How'd you find out about us?"

"An ad in the paper"

"Great! Do you like round or rectangular better?"

"Round."

"How many people do you usually seat?"

"Four."

"We have that over here."

Then I take them to what they described and give them a presentation on the features and benefits of that particular table. The presentation part will be in the next chapter.

Why

Always start by saying "Hi". The customers will usually respond back with "Hi". Anything else, especially "How are you doing?" makes it easier for the customer to respond "Just looking".

About half the time the customers would tell you what they were looking for after you said "Yes, sir?" Then you start narrowing down their choices. About half the time they would say, "Just looking". Then you would continue on with the "Oh, okay. What were you looking for?" Most of them would then tell you what it was. I'll explain how to handle the few that continued to say, "just looking" later on in this chapter.

Of course if it's a single woman, say, "Yes ma'am?" But in the couples the man is more likely to tell you what they're looking for. The woman in the couple will be much more likely to say, "Just looking". Once he says what they're looking for, then devote your questions to the woman. She is less likely to tell you what they're looking for, but she's the one making the decision in most retail situations. So sell her. Don't be rude and ignore the man, but devote all your questions to her if possible. Sell her and you'll sell him.

When you're taking customers towards what they're looking for, you want to lead them. It's important you take the lead, because that shows you are in control of the group. I found I could predict pretty accurately if a salesperson was going to make a sale just by noticing this without even eavesdropping on the sale. If the salesperson was leading the group around the store, a sale was probably going to be made. If the customer was leading the salesperson around, a sale probably wouldn't be made.

As you are walking toward the items they're looking for, then ask, "How did you find out about us?" This gives you more of an idea of whom you're dealing with while getting them comfortable conversing with you. If they are a referral, or a repeat customer, they're already pretty sold. If they just saw the ad, they'll be a little tougher. Also you'll find out if someone has been in before so you'll know whether to alter your presentation a little so it won't sound canned. Again, if the woman is bringing her husband back, you've pretty much got a sale. If he's bringing her back to see what he saw, it'll be tougher and you really have to concentrate on her. In any case, if they tell you they found out about your store by ad or referral or are coming back a second time, they are seriously looking for something to fill a need. That way you can be very matter of fact when you ask your next questions without seeming pushy or weird.

These words work great only if said in the right way at the right place and time. Let's move on now to how to find the right place in your store.

TWO
Where to Stand and Why

Now that you know what to say when the customers come in, you need to find where you should be when they come in. It's not good to be right next to the door as that intimidates people. When they get intimidated, they get nervous. You want them relaxed. If you notice, they usually turn to the right or go straight ahead when they enter the store. Observe the natural traffic pattern in your store. You want to be close enough to the door so that when they come in you can greet them with a cheery "Hi", and make eye contact. You also don't want to be too far from where they usually stop.

The ideal place for you to stand is about fifteen to twenty feet from the door. This way you won't crowd customers as they come in. When you study the traffic pattern of your store, you'll notice that most of the time they will come in and stop in the same couple of places. These will usually be either to their right or straight ahead. You don't want to be there to disrupt the natural traffic pattern, but be able to walk toward them fairly quickly when they stop.

Why

If you greet them while they are still walking, they know what they are going to do next, which is take a step. It doesn't matter what you say or how you say it, they'll say, "just looking." This means wait for them to stop. Don't interrupt them. Some people walk farther than others, and I've seen one or two that never stopped from the moment they walked in until they left. But it's all right. Don't bother greeting them until they've stopped. Again, this was all learned from years of trial and error.

If you greet them after they have stopped and resumed walking, they will usually say, "just looking" no matter what you say or how you say it. Again the reason is they know what they're going to do next.

Timing is everything: the reason you wait for them to stop is because this is the moment when they don't know what to do next. Since they are unsure of where to go, they are off-balance and vulnerable. Their mind is occupied with what to do next. This moment of indecision is the perfect time to come up confidently and help them out by taking control. When this is done right, you're on your way to being their friend and adviser.

THREE
How to Stand and Why

If it is your turn to help the next customer that comes in, it's good to be alone doing something mindless like dusting when they come in. That way you'll be busy, but your mind can still be on sales. Don't be doing something that requires serious concentration.

Why

It's less stressful for your customers if you look occupied when they come in. Dusting is a good mindless thing to do and also shows that you value your merchandise. If you're just waiting by the door for the next customer to appear, it makes them feel like the prey while you look like the predator. You don't want them thinking you're trying to sell them something. You want them to think you're a good guy who knows a lot about your product. Remember, keep it as relaxed as possible.

There is another reason you want to be alone and not talking to other sales people when the customer comes in. Think about it. If a stranger walks into a public room where a group of people who know each other are talking, it's not natural to suddenly have one person from that group leave the others and start talking to the stranger. Of course it's even worse if it is a group of salespeople. It is normal and polite for a stranger to walk into a room where one person is by himself and for that person to greet the stranger and strike up a conversation with him or her.

When I worked the store by myself and there were no customers, I would be reading. When I heard a car pull up, I would get up and act like I was working on a piece of furniture, putting a table together, sanding something, etc. Then when customers came in, they would think I was more a craftsman than a salesman, so they had more confidence in what I said. People trust a mechanic's opinion on cars more than a car salesman's. It also didn't make it look like I was just there waiting for them to come in so I could pounce on them. It's a stage, it's theatre! It's fun!

The most intimidating thing you can do is to have all the salespeople behind desks facing the door or all congregated in one spot on the floor like the counter. If there's more than one salesperson working, it's best to keep the ones waiting their turn out of sight. We used to have a back lunchroom with a door bell that was rung from the front counter by someone every time a customer came in so the next salesperson would then know to come out.

When it got so busy that all the salespeople were occupied, we would have someone from another department watch the door for us. He would have a piece of paper and write down a description of the customers that came in when there were no salespeople available to take them: "lady in blue hat", "couple with child", whatever. Then when a salesperson was finished with his customer, he would ask the door watcher to point out who needed help. This eliminated the embarrassing times when a salesperson would greet a customer that another salesperson was already helping. Maybe the customer was walking around thinking about a purchase or had asked the salesperson to find an item that was not on the floor. Customers get annoyed if several salespeople hit on them, especially with the exact same greeting.

FOUR
How to Say It and Why

When customers first come in, make eye contact and say, "Hi", but that's all. Don't say, "How are you" or anything else, because that makes it easy to respond with "Oh, just looking". "Hi" is safe. Don't move after you say "Hi". Instead, wait for your customers to stop. That's when you move toward them. Approach them with confidence. When you get to where they are stopped say "Yes, sir?" Accent the "sir", not the "yes". Raise your voice on the "sir" so it sounds like a question. Be confident, not shy or hesitant. Look them in the eye the whole time. Half the time they will tell you what they are looking for. Half the time they'll say, "We're just looking". If they say "just looking", say, "Oh, okay. What were you looking for?" While saying these lines your body language should be non-threatening. Clasp your hands behind your back, drop your shoulders, make your eyes as big as you can and nod your head when you say, "Okay". Pause a second or two between "okay" and "what". Then ask what they were looking for. Most of the time they will tell you. This will work for about ninety per cent of the people that come in if you do it exactly as I say. We'll discuss how to handle the ten per cent that say "just looking" a second time later in this chapter.

Why

The reason the "Yes, sir?" works is because you catch them when they don't know what they're going to do next. That's why they have stopped. It takes them by surprise, and often they tell you what they're looking for. It's crisp, professional, no-nonsense and to the point. They usually respond in kind. People are mirrors of you. If you're hesitant, shy, or indecisive, they usually will be too.

If you put the accent on the "sir", it will work. If you put the accent on the "yes", it won't. We had a woman work for us who was very good at sales, especially sofas. I told her about the "Yes sir?" greeting and how it was quick, easy, and efficient. Everyone she used it on told her they were just looking. We tried and tried to figure out why it didn't work for her while it almost always worked for me. Finally we figured it out. While observing her, I noticed that she was accenting the "yes" and not the "sir". Coming out with a strong "yes" just about knocks the customer over. You want to accent the "sir". It sounds more like a question. Accenting the "yes" sounds like a response to a military officer. Come to think of it, her husband was in the military. Sales is word art. Everything has to be done right.

The "Oh, Okay" works because when they say "Just looking", they are in effect throwing up a wall. When you agree and say "Oh, okay", they relax and the wall comes down. Then when you ask what they were looking for, you'll get a straight answer. If you forget the "Oh, okay", or say "Oh, okay. What were you looking for?" too fast, without enough pause between "Okay" and "What" that wall is still up and you're going to bounce right off it! They'll say, "I said I was just looking!" Whoops!

Now that you understand the timing, voice inflections and positioning involved in the greeting, this is a good time for you to go back and review the sample greeting script.

Still Just Looking!

But what if the customer says "Just looking" on the second try? Then say pleasantly and nonchalantly, "Okay." and immediately turn around and leave. Give them what they don't expect. The reason they say, "just looking" is to get rid of you. They expect you to hang around them and be pushy and say inappropriate things, following and watching them every step of the way, It's unnatural.

If you say, "Okay" and turn immediately away, you've taken this worry away from them and they can relax a little around you. You'll find a lot of times as soon as you turn around and take a couple of steps away from them, they'll call back for you and ask where a particular item is. Then go back and take control. Say, "They're this way". Then lead them to it. They asked you to be there. It's natural.

One thing that's hard not to do is tell them the layout of your store when they say "just looking" a second time. You're geared to be as helpful as you can, but you need to hold back that urge. For example, sometimes the customer says, "just looking" and the salesperson responds, "We have bedrooms upstairs, tables and chairs there." You do that, and they really don't need you at all. They said they were just looking, and now they know where everything is to look at. If you go up to them again, you're going to seem pushy. You have to wait for them to come get you. Fat chance. Remember they came into look on their own, study the item, and go home and think about it.

If they say "just looking" twice and don't ask where something is, you will have to wait and hope they stop and study an item for a while. Don't follow them around. If you haven't seen them for a while, send a spy, someone who is not busy, to look for them. Then they can report back to you as to what they're doing.

If they're stopped and are studying an item for a while, then go up to them and tell the customers a fact about the item. Don't state the obvious, but say, "That comes bigger or smaller, too." Or let them know that it comes lighter or darker, or that it's discontinued. Don't start giving them a presentation on the item they're looking at or give them a feature and benefit of it. Many times I did that and then found out they weren't looking for that particular item. For example they would be studying a sofa for a while. I'd walk up and give a presentation on it. They would listen patiently then tell me they were really looking for tables. This makes you look really out of touch to them, and it makes your presentations sound canned. Besides, you only want to give a presentation on what they are looking for. Too many presentations will confuse them. I'll get into this more in the next chapter.

Once you have stated a fact about the item they were studying, you have to hope that they ask you a question to keep you there. If they say "just looking" again, you're out. You've got three strikes. Now there's no way you can go back to them without seeming pushy. They've told you they were just looking three times, for God's sake. Now they'll tell all their friends your store is full of pushy salespeople. Surely you've heard them complain about other stores being that way. Don't give your store that reputation. I had a customer complaining to me about a competitor's salesman following them right on their heels. They were confiding this to me while I was right on their heels. I found that strange but they never noticed it. That's how relaxed they were around me!

At this point you can let another salesperson try. You have nothing to lose. You've already lost. Even if they have a question, they probably won't ask you just out of pride. Since they've blown you off three times, they're embarrassed to come after you now. It could give you an opportunity to gloat: "See, I knew you needed me!" And they normally would rather not do that. They'll ask someone else if they really want to know something.

Once you've told a new salesperson to try them, they should do it this way. The salesperson should walk by them while doing something, like carrying a chair or something to another part of the store. In passing, they should smile and say "Hi" in a real friendly way. It's good to make a comment about the weather or the customers' children. After dropping off the chair, the salesperson should come back by the customers and ask, "What were you looking for?" If they say just looking again, forget it. This doesn't happen much. But when it does, the only way you still have a chance to sell them something is not to alienate them. If you approach them one more time, you're going to make them angry. You simply have to hope they come to someone and ask for help. You have done all you can do. You have to know your limitations.

Conclusion

So you can see how important it is to perfect your greeting. Your greeting allows you to take control of the sale and find out what the customer wants. Once you have control, you can keep it right through the close step. If you don't take control in the beginning, you're merely just "there", trusting your livelihood to luck. If you've got bills to pay, that can be hard. A polished greeting takes the sale out of Lady Luck's hands and puts it back in yours.

Chapter Six

Step Two: The Presentation

The presentation is when you give the customer the facts and benefits of your product. I'll show you how to write presentations later in this chapter. Good presentations were a big key to our success. If you read any outside sales book, it will tell you to use presentations. They make it easier to close a sale. If you use them in a retail setting, the results are phenomenal.

When I was training new salespeople, I would first bring them to the table and give them the presentation on it. They would listen and be impressed with the table. I would then show them the table presentation in our presentation book. They would always be amazed that everything I had just said was already written down word for word. It had seemed so spontaneous and natural! Presentations are a listing of facts and benefits. You tell the customer a fact, then immediately tell them how it benefits them. There are a million facts you can say about a wood table: where the wood is from, the religion of the maker, etc. Only give the facts that have a direct benefit to the customer. A good rule of thumb is to list three facts and benefits. If you are constantly getting a certain objection to the item, you want to include a fact benefit that answers this objection. That way you eliminate the objection before it comes up. That is the best way to handle objections - answer them before they come up.

To help make it clearer what we're talking about, here is a sample presentation on an oak pedestal t.able that we used for years. In fact it was our first presentation.

Oak Pedestal Table

"This is our oak pedestal table here. The only thing different on it is on the legs down here. Each one is adjustable. You can raise or lower each leg about a third of an inch. That way if your floor isn't level, you can adjust the high leg down so it won't wobble. Because it's the D.C. area, the same finish that goes on top goes underneath. That seals the wood from quick changes in humidity, which this area has, and that's hard on unfinished wood. When the wood is sealed the moisture can't get in and bother it. The top is a third thicker than most. Most are 3/4" thick. This is an inch thick. It's all solid oak, which is about your hardest wood, so it lasts a long time. Now a table like this finished dark or golden is $235.00. (Pause.)

How long have you been looking for a table?"

The customer will then reply with how long they've been looking.

"This price is less than what similar tables cost that aren't made as well."

That's it. You can see what I mean about fact benefit and answering objections. A lot of people were leery of this kind of table because they were afraid it would wobble on the floor. You tell them the fact about the adjustable legs, then the benefit that the table will set solid on any floor. This eliminates the wobbling objection.

48

Customers were also afraid of warping. You give them the fact that the table is finished underneath as well as on top. Then you give them the benefit of this. Changes in humidity won't affect it. This eliminated the objection to warping and splitting. It also made it seem like it was custom-made for the D.C. area.

Giving them the fact that it was a thick oak table then let you give them the benefit that it would last a long time. Some people were afraid that it was hard to take care of wood and that it was fragile compared to Formica or something like that. This got rid of that objection.

So that's an example of a presentation and the reasons for saying each part. Every item you sell has at least three fact- benefits you can tell about it. Preferably the presentation answers a common objection, like the legs wobbling or warping table tops in the case of the table.

Sales presentations are important for many reasons. One is they answer the main objections to your product before the customer brings them up. This is better than answering the objections as the customer brings them up. In sales you want to stay ahead of the customer. You don't want to be defensive or playing catch up.

The first day that I went out selling I was on the side of the main road at a gas station. The owner let us set up on his property by the roadside. We had great oak porch rockers that were cheap, strong, and comfortable, plus, everyone wanted them. Even though we were the only ones who had them, I couldn't sell them. I'd tell them how it was made. They would sit in them and like them. The price was good. Then they would say it's too bad they put that metal angle brace under the arm and wouldn't buy the rocker because of it.

I got really frustrated. So finally when I was giving the rocker presentation to them, I added this. I went through the whole presentation and then said," And the only things that aren't old style are these braces under the arms. They put them there because that's the first place they break. Little kids sit on them. And some people hang their leg over them. With the braces there, nothing happens. And that's the whole idea behind this kind of furniture. Just a simple, rugged rocker that you can leave outside and not have to worry about it!" I sold all I had after I started saying that. Nobody ever mentioned or objected to the braces after that. So that's an example of how you answer objections before they come up. It works so much better!

I found out later that all porch rockers had this brace under the arm. Porch rockers have no glue in them so the rain won't dissolve the glue. The reason for the brace is really a technical issue. Since customers weren't aware that all porch rockers have them, I was able to turn their initial objection into a selling point that made our rocker seem special.

Another thing the presentation does is build up desire in the customer for the product. It goes from being just a table to a really great table that's worth more than its price. When the desire is built up, you get less vague answers to your questions as now the customer is really interested and less guarded. You also appear very knowledgeable about your product so the customer trusts your opinion more. Plus, if you're the only store doing good presentations on your products and your competition is just winging it and gun shy from all the customers saying they're just looking, you'll get a great reputation for quality and a knowledgeable sales staff. That's what we did. Over the years we made the Washingtonian Magazine and the Baltimore Magazine's best buys issue.

There is one other thing about building up their desire. Only give the presentation on what they're interested in. Presentations are very powerful and can make the customer want the item. If you give it on everything, they'll want everything. But they can't afford it. So they get nothing because they have to go home and think about what they want to get.

I learned this the hard way. A couple came in and wanted a table and chairs. They told me they had five hundred dollars to spend. I gave them the presentation on a table and chairs that added up to five hundred dollars. They liked it, now they wanted to see the rest of the store before they decided. They really liked a five hundred dollar corner cabinet. I gave them a presentation on it. Then they left. They couldn't decide whether to spend their five hundred dollars on a table and chairs or a corner cabinet. This was a no brainer to me. Since they just moved in with no furniture, they would get much more immediate use from a table and chairs. It was either have a place to eat every day or have a nice place to store dishes. The dishes could stay in a regular cabinet for a while.

They finally came back a year later and got the table and chairs. That's when I realized how powerful the presentations were! So only give them a presentation on what the customers said they were looking for in the greeting. That way when they look at what else you have in the store, everything seems nice, but the thing that stands out as really nice is the item you gave the presentation on. And that also happens to be the item they have an immediate need for. Imagine that! After they buy that, then sell them on other stuff they said they had an interest in later.

The third thing a rehearsed presentation does is free your mind to concentrate on the customer instead of thinking about what you're going to say next, because you've got it memorized cold. You can read their reactions to what you're saying and avoid being oblivious to their reaction to you or the product. Thinking about what you are going to say next instead of concentrating on the customer's reactions is a major reason a lot of salespeople come across as insensitive. All outside sales people use presentations for these reasons and they work. Outside sales are tougher than in-store sales, and you have to be quick witted. You can't be quick witted when you are thinking about what to say next. Your mind has to be free to be in the moment and increase your sales.

Presentations have a bad reputation among salespeople, though. They say they are corny and sound canned. They're corny for two reasons. Many times the people who wrote them never sold the product. They just wrote what they thought would work without actually doing it. Or they were written by people who did it a long time ago, but manners of speaking and the customer's attitude have changed since then.

You eliminate that by writing down only what you've been saying for a while that has good results.

There was only so much you could say about an oak pedestal table to customer after customer before you noticed that you were repeating yourself. If you say a phrase that has a good effect, keep saying it. If you say a phrase that doesn't have a good effect, or confuses people, quit saying it.

So, get in the habit of writing down what you've been saying whenever you've had a successful sale. That way your new people can start right out saying the right thing, instead of learning it by trial and error like you did. If they're smart, it's what they're going to end up saying anyway.

A presentation will sound canned whenever the salesperson was too lazy to memorize it cold before he went out on the floor. We would have people memorize a presentation. They would then recite it to me in a small room. It didn't matter how they said it. The only thing that mattered was that they knew it. It was hard to recite it to me for two reasons. It was an unnatural situation, just sitting there in a small room, plus I already knew what they were supposed to say. The pressure was on!

Saying it to the customer was much easier. It was a natural setting, plus the customer didn't know what you were supposed to say. When you know it cold, it sounds like a normal conversation. If you could say it under the hardest of conditions, you could say it anywhere. If you couldn't say it under the hardest conditions, there were probably other places you couldn't say it either. Don't cut yourself any slack. You don't have to be theatrical or rhythmic in your delivery in practice. You just have to be able to say it word for word to someone who already knows what you're supposed to say. If you can do that, you can do it anywhere to anybody. Then you add the theatrics and rhythm. The total amount of time it took to recite the table presentation and the close was about a minute and a half. But the sale would last anywhere from a half-hour to two hours! This helped salespeople to understand that most of the sale was asking questions and then listening intently.

I read an interview of a sports coach one time. Sales is a lot like sports because it's your ability on that day that counts. You've got to be in the moment. He said you want to make all of your mistakes in practice where it doesn't count. Don't let things slide while practicing in private or you will be making mistakes when it counts. It's too late then. When you go out on the field, you'd better know what you're doing. Because when you go out to perform, you want to be relaxed and in a good mood. If you don't know your presentations very well, you won't be relaxed. I used to read comic books I liked before going out on the floor so I would be relaxed and happy. Basically, you just give the presentation and be yourself when you're on the floor.

Also like sports, once you have them memorized, you want to review them periodically. Pro football players have been playing since they were kids, yet they still practice everyday. Once you're sharp, you have to stay sharp. It's all about today, not yesterday!

My partner got to the point where he would only sell periodically. But when he did, he would always do well. He told me his secret was to review the presentation for about fifteen minutes before he went on the floor. Then he would just give the presentation and be himself while giving it. He wasn't as good as people who sold all the time, but he still sold most of the people he talked to.

If you are a sales manager having salespeople reciting the presentations to you, you should only tell them what they did wrong after they've finished. Don't correct people as they make a mistake. They're nervous enough without having to worry the manager is going to jump in with criticism at any time. It's also good for the manager to look at the floor and not at the person reciting. Staring at the person reciting makes them nervous also. It's nerve-wracking enough for first timers. No need to add to it, unless for some reason the manager feels he made a mistake in hiring the person. If you stare at them while they are trying to recite it, they'll get flustered and frustrated and understand when you tell them it's not going to work out.

The presentations are to be memorized cold so you don't have to think about what you're going to say next. It comes out without thinking. That frees your mind so you can concentrate on the customer. You can observe the customer's reactions to yourself and the product. Presentations help make you a much more sensitive sales person. If you're constantly winging it each time a customer comes in, your mind is preoccupied with what you're going to say next. You're not concentrating on the customer. That's where salespeople get the reputation of being insensitive.

So as you can see, these objections to presentations are not valid. It's just that the people who wrote them or the people who memorized them didn't do it right. After you start using them the right way, you'll never want to go without them again. You'll feel naked or unarmed.

Another rule in doing a good presentation is don't start out saying that this is a great table because. Say, "The only thing different on this from most is..." You want them to listen to you. You can talk all day long and if they're not listening, so what? If you start out saying it's great because, they figure you're just going to say good things to try to sell them, so they tune you out because they don't want to be talked into something they don't want to do. If you say, "The only thing different on this from most...", they don't know if you're going to say something good or bad about it, so they listen.

When giving the presentation, always look the customers in the eye. It's more natural to look at your hands while they're pointing at the features but don't. You want to be able to read how the customers are reacting to what you're saying. If they are interested, bored, confused etc. The customers will watch your hands pointing out the features, but every once in a while they will look at you. When they do, they'll be looking into your eyes, not the side of your face. This also connotes sincerity.

Watching the customers also avoids embarrassing moments where the salesperson is talking and watching his hands and can't notice that the customer isn't paying attention or in some cases has even walked away! I've seen both before.

The other thing is that the eyes are like magnets. When you give the table presentation and are at the point when you say "...the legs down here..." you crouch down to point at the legs. Keep looking them in the eye and they will crouch down with you. Don't say another thing until they are down. Now they are really listening because they've invested physical effort into what you're saying. Don't say another word until they're down because they will realize they can listen to you without crouching and rise back up. Once they're down, they're down. Now you have their rapt attention.

It works because the eyes are very powerful. Eye contact keeps them there. If the couple looks like they want to back away, especially the woman, never take your eyes off hers. I had a situation like that once and it really worked. During my presentation she would take a half step back periodically. I kept looking her in the eye the whole time. Then she would take a half step toward me. Back and forth it went. Half way through the presentation she came up to the table and me. Had I broken eye contact once, even for a second, she would have been gone and missed the whole presentation.

As you point out features on the table, touch it with love and respect and they will too. Of course the more they touch it, the more they want it. Also, it's good to nod your head yes periodically while you're making your points to them. They'll do the same, and that's what you want them to get in the habit of doing - saying yes. Try to make your eyes big since that is a comforting and sincere way of talking. You seem less threatening.

Once you have the presentation memorized, don't say it in a monotone. Raise and lower your voice in a nice cadence. This helps lull the customer into a trance. Remember that they're people, not computers. Good speech making is an art. Auctioneers have to go to school to learn the craft. They tap their feet to a steady rhythm and keep their speech to that rhythm. You sell more if you talk in a rhythm. Try not to talk fast or they'll think you're a fast talker. Slow connotes honesty.

So that's it on the presentation. Once you get used to using them, you'll never want to wing it again. There is just no comparison between the two. Just write and memorize them in the right way. You'll love the difference! Next we'll get into "How long have you been looking?"

Chapter Seven

Step Three: How Long Have You Been Looking?

When you reach the end of any presentation, pause and then ask, "How long have you been looking for a (blank)?" In response to whatever answer they give, say, "Our price is less than most of this quality and design". They will usually agree with you on this point. After all the great things you just told them about this product, of course they would expect to pay more! By getting them to say it's a good deal, you've reinforced it in their mind. It also makes them more forthright to your questions. We'll get into the main question and answer period in more detail in the next chapter.

The customers will usually start asking you specific questions about the product. If they don't, then you start asking them questions to narrow down what exactly they want. You do this step for two reasons. First, you find out how long they've been looking so you know how much knowledge they have to compare your product with others. You're learning more about whom you're dealing with here. If they just started or this is the first place, they're going to be harder to sell. If they've been looking two weeks to two months, they'll be easier. But you have to ask it exactly as I've written it. If you say, "Have you been looking long?" they will almost always say, "No, not long". Even if it's been two months, a year, it doesn't matter.

Always ask questions that will give you specific answers, not vague ones. Is there, was there, would there etc. are not good ways to start questions in sales. You're making it too easy for them to say no or nothing. Ask questions that start with what, how, when, or why. These words will get you specific answers, which is what you need in order to sell them. Customers are prepared to say "not long". But when you make them give the time, if it's over two weeks, you can see it in their face as they speak it that they can't believe it's taking this long. It puts them in the frame of mind to get it over with. That's the frame of mind you want!

Nothing about human behavior is one hundred per cent. Usually two to three weeks is long enough for most people to look around for furniture and feel they have a pretty good handle on what's available. Some people, like government workers, feel you can never explore enough options, and two months doesn't seem like a long time. Others, like salespeople, think one day is enough time to be sure of what's out there.

The other thing this step does is to get them started talking and answering your questions. They'll be in a better frame of mind now to give you straight answers. You've talked enough, now it's their turn to talk. A good salesperson is not so much a good talker as he is a good listener. If you time yourself, it only takes about a minute and a half to say a presentation, but a sale lasts usually from thirty minutes to two hours. The rest of the time is you asking questions to narrow down the customers' choice so you can close them. Ask questions and listen, and they will tell you what they want. You can't sell someone who doesn't talk. If they interrupt you, shut up immediately and listen. Be thankful they're talking. Remember the last customer you had that wouldn't talk or even acknowledge you. You can't sell them. If you're lucky, at the end they'll say they want to buy something, but it's just luck.

If the answer they give to how long they've been looking is an inordinate amount of time like a year or so, there's something going on. Usually that means they don't really need it. If they say a year or a long time, ask, "What are you using now?" Usually they'll say it's adequate, and they're just looking for a great deal that will make replacing it worthwhile. A lot of times they saw exactly what they want somewhere. It's perfect. It's just too expensive or a one of a kind that was already sold. They know what they want. They're looking for the exact same thing, only cheaper. But it has to be exactly the same. In the meantime, the one they have now works just fine.

The first time someone told me they'd been looking for a year, I got all excited because I thought they'd be easy to sell. I mean, everyone who'd been looking two weeks to two months knew it was good. I thought the more they had looked, the better it was for me. Well, they were the toughest. It took several visits by them to the barn before they bought. Before these people came to the barn, I had a hundred per cent closing rate. Anyone who saw you on the street and took the time to come out and see what you had in the barn was serious. These guys messed up my average. Right after they bought it, they got a divorce. I guess looking for a table and chairs was what was holding the marriage together.

Another time I saw this phenomenon from the inside. A lady worked for us whose husband was in the Air Force and was stationed near here for three years. He wanted a new van and she didn't. He would go out and look at new vans by himself. Then he would bring her to the lot and show her. He wanted to buy. This was obvious for the salesman to see, and I'm sure he could taste the sale. The wife would go along up until the moment of truth, then give her husband a look and say, "Let's think about it." She would then get him to stop looking for a while, explaining they didn't have the money or something like that, Time would go on and he would go out looking again. I watched this through her eyes for three years. It was then I realized the salesman would ask him how long he'd been looking and he would say three years and the salesman would think that surely he's going to crack now. It must have been very frustrating for the unthinking salesman who was just taking all this at face value. Of course, the big rule in retail selling is that the woman is the one who makes the final decision. She is the one who must be sold.

My car salesman friend said there are two reasons people don't buy, the reason they tell you and the real reason. So this is why when they say they've been looking an abnormally long time, you want to ask what they're using now. The more information you can get the better. Always ask questions and listen intently, looking them in the eye the whole time. Listening is a lost art. Most people don't do it well. If you listen to them, you'll probably be one of the few in their lives who does. So even if you don't know them, you will be special in their eyes as someone who listens to them.

People really crave that. Of course always keep the conversation on the sale, not other subjects.

Now you know what type of item they're looking for and how long they have been looking for it. You've gotten them interested in it enough to answer your questions straight. And you know how much they have to compare it too. Now it's time to narrow down exactly what they want.

Chapter Eight

Step Four: What Exactly Do They Want?

I think this is the hardest of the steps because there's no real formula other than asking questions, knowing the answers to common objections, and using your own wits to answer the uncommon objections. Remember to ask questions that will give you specific answers. Start them out with what, when, where, how, and why, not was there, is there, etc.

You'll find that there are certain objections that come up fairly frequently. The ones that come up all the time are the ones you want to incorporate into your presentation. The other ones that come up only sometimes you want to figure out an answer that shows the customers that this objection of theirs is not a problem. We would write down the common objections with the answers and review them periodically.

When you answer an objection to not buying, it's good to make it seem like a spontaneous part of the conversation, not an automatic memorized answer. Show respect for the customers' intelligence, and don't dismiss the objection as stupid. Nicely explain why it's not a problem, but show you understand why they would think it is. Make sure they save face. The uncommon and one of a kind objections you have to figure out on the spot. You have to be on your toes and quick witted. This is why to sell you have to be intelligent.

Another reason this is a hard step is that most people don't like to make decisions, even about things that they know. You're trying to get them to make a decision in a strange place about something they probably don't know much about. This is hard to do! Realize this and act accordingly. This is why you want to be their knowledgeable friend and adviser. They'll feel more comfortable making a decision with you.

In reviewing sales with sales people, this is the step they usually skipped. You know if you skipped it because the customer will have to go home and measure, decide what size, color, style, etc. This is what you want to avoid. It's easy to skip the completion of this step, but it doesn't go away. It just comes back to haunt you in the close.

In a nutshell it goes something like this.

Salesperson: "Which color table do you like?"

Customer: "The dark."

Salesperson: "What size do you prefer?"

Customer: "I like the 48, *but I'm not sure it would fit*. What other kinds of chairs do you have?"

Salesperson: "They're right here"

Customer: "I like these chairs."

Salesperson: "How many of these chairs did you want?"

Customer: "I want four chairs and a round table in this color."

Salesperson: "When did you want them?"

Customer: "Three weeks."

Salesperson: Explains close.

Customer: "That sounds great! I have to go home and measure and I'll be back!"

They're gone. If you're having trouble getting them to decide on a particular variable, don't move on. Stay there until it's done. As soon as you close someone without knowing exactly what the person wants, they are going to bring up the fact that they still haven't decided what they want yet and you've just made it a lot easier for them to leave and "think about it." So why close them? When you close them, you are asking them to buy something. But what are you asking them to buy if they don't know what they want yet? You have to stay on this step until it's done.

Sometimes this is the last step of your sale. If there is no way you can get them to decide, you're better off going with the odds and letting them walk. They respect you more. I've written orders for a dark or gold finish 48" table. Most of the time they canceled. I think the reason was that they looked at the order, and saw one or the other. I looked like I was desperate for a sale. Then they wonder why I am so desperate. They think that maybe most people aren't buying this stuff for a good reason they don't know. They get scared, and you lose the sale.

If the customers aren't sure of the size of the table they need, I found this to work. I'd say, "If the bigger one fits, that's the one you'd rather have, right?" They'd say yes. I'd say, "To save you a trip, I'll write the order for the bigger one. You go home and measure. If the big one fits, fine. If you want the smaller one, my name is Terry, I'm here until six. Call me and I'll change it to the

67

smaller size. That way you don't have to come back, and what you want will be here when you're ready for it".

Always write the order for the item they prefer. That way a lot of times they don't bother to call. Don't write it for the one they really don't prefer. Make it easy for them. This way only one item appears on the receipt. When they read it in the privacy of their home, you don't look as desperate. Of course, you can apply this method to other things like color, style, etc.

Now, that I have given you an idea of how to salvage an uncertain sale, I'll give you some techniques that will make it a cleaner sale in the first place. You want the type of sale that will make you proud and not look like a rookie. The real life examples I am giving are for furniture. But these ideas can be adapted to anything if you think about it.

The first rule is to treat every customer as if they are very hard to sell. Follow all the rules I've laid out. That way you're ready. If they're easy, it'll be easy. If they're hard, you're ready for them. If you start out as though they're going to be an easy sale and they're easy, you're all right. If they're hard, you're sunk. You can't play catch-up in sales. You've got to stay ahead of customers. You've got to stay in control. Remember, if they're in control, they're going to go home and think about it.

In the greeting you asked them which wood and style table they liked. Then you gave them a presentation on that style. Now you need to know the color and size. When asking which color people like, it's good to say, "Which color do you usually prefer?" Everybody knows what color they usually prefer. If you ask which color did they like better, you're leaving yourself open to the "I don't know response."

Talk about the size of the table in terms of how many people they usually sit, not the actual size of the table. Everybody knows how many people they usually sit. Not all of them know what size will fit into their room. Then they have to go home and measure. Make it easy for them to make a decision in the store.

Table sizes have a formula for how many people they sit. On a round table, after 18" in diameter to start with, every six inches is a person. In other words, a 36" table will seat three comfortably and up to four, a 42" table four to five, a 48" five to six. So instead of referring to the tables in terms of inches, refer to them as to how many people they seat. When you are showing them how many people can eat around the table, sit in the chair at the table. Then get up without moving the chair. It will be back a foot or two from the table so that you can fit between the chair and the table. Most customers will want to put the chairs as close as possible to the table when trying to see how many people can fit around it. It's not accurate so always show it as the chairs will be with people on them! You'll get more chairs around it that way.

If they say they usually sit four people, say, "This table is 42" and is made to seat four all the time five, once in a while." Then explain the formula. That makes it official and usually takes their worry away about which size to get. Always go with the smallest table that will fit their needs. If they want to go to a bigger one, that's great. But if they say they have to measure, you can say, "Well if this doesn't fit, this is the smallest table in this style we have that will seat the people you want to. If this doesn't fit, you may want to try another style." Rectangular and oval tables also increase in size to add more people, not take up more space. The products you sell probably have a reason for their variables too. Know what they are!

The thing you want to avoid is having them go home and measure. If you talk in terms of measurements, that's probably going to happen. You have control over what's talked about. You got it in the greeting. So don't say something that's going to shoot yourself in the foot.

On tables, always ask how many they usually seat, not how many they want to seat. They may want a table to seat twenty once a year, four the rest of the year. I've asked, "How many people do you want to seat?" and got stuck looking for a table that seated twenty, and of course there was no way it fit in their room, or it was far too expensive. You can try to get out of this mess by then asking, "How many people do you seat at it most of the time?" Then you can say, "This will do what you want it to do 364 days out of the year. One day out of 365 you'll have to make do. That's better than having a table that's right one day out of 365, and having a table that's too big 364 days out of the year". But as always it's better to avoid this problem altogether.

I've noticed on the tables when I ask "How many people do you usually seat?", I can see they're all set to give me the number they want to seat once in a while, then they realize the question and give me the normal number.

If they're having trouble deciding between two styles, colors, etc. put the two next to each other in front of the customer. While you're doing this say, "Here, this will make it easier for you to decide." Then step back and wait. Don't say, "This might make it easier" etc. Say, "This will make it easier." That way they don't have an out. If you say "It might make it easier", they can say, "Thanks but it doesn't work." By being positive and saying, "This will make it easier", they are embarrassed if they can't make up their mind. You always assume the sale.

The other key is silence after you do this. Wait for them to say something. Silence is the highest form of pressure. Now the only way out for the customers is to say something. And that something has to be a decision. The silence is as uncomfortable for you as it is for them. Just when you feel you must say something, count to ten. Usually before you get there, they'll say something. If not, count again, but this usually isn't necessary. If you say something before they do, like, "They're nice aren't they?", they'll say, "Yes, but I still can't make up my mind." You just gave them an out. Don't do that.

Whatever decision the customers finally make, reassure them it was a good choice. They need to know this to erase all doubts. Don't feel hypocritical about this. It's a free country, so it's good for them to get what they want. Wait until they definitely say they like one before you reassure them on their choice. Sometimes when they were picking out chairs, they would say, "This one feels nice." Then thirty seconds later they would say "But I like this one better." So wait until you're sure which one they want before you reassure them.

If you say, "That is a nice style", and then they say, "But I like the other one better", good luck. Now what do you say? "I was just kidding. I think that one's better too". See, if you sell the way I'm telling you, they will look at you as an expert on your product and not just another salesperson. What you say will carry real weight. Then they get confused about what to buy because they want one thing, but the expert says another is better. No one does what they don't want to do, so they usually won't buy anything.

Everything you sell should be a good value, so what ever they buy will do them fine. Your job is to help them find out what they want. Then your job is to reassure them that it is alright for them to get what they want. Boom, you've made them happy. And they'll keep coming back to you for future needs because you make them happy. And to me, that's a fun job.

When the time comes to decide on chairs and they want to see what a particular chair looks like at the table, put a whole set of chairs around the table. The first impression is what they see. Make it a good one. One chair at a table usually looks small and unimpressive. A whole set doesn't. Don't just put one up to the table. The customer will say he only needs one at the table to decide. Say, "No problem, this will give you a more accurate view" and bring up a set of at least four. Bring two chairs up to the table and set them beside the table. Then bring the other two up. Now put them all around at the same time. Presto! It looks great!

If they offer to help you bring the chairs up to the table, that's good. Say, "Our prices are good because we put you to work." They usually laugh. Remember, the more they touch the item and get involved in the sale, the more they are likely to buy. Just make sure you get to the table with your two chairs first so you can wait for them. Then when they get there you put all the chairs around it at the same time.

Also the more you do to help them make a decision, the more likely they'll be to buy. Don't be lazy. Work for the sale. Show them attention. If they are trying to decide between two items, bring them together. Don't have the customer walk back and forth between the two items. It takes too long and is not as effective. We had an excellent sales woman work for us and that was her trademark. She'd have stuff rearranged all over the store. But she almost always got the sale. Not only are you making it easier for them to decide, they appreciate the extra service and attention. It's a pretty safe bet that you're one of the few salespeople they've had who does this much to make it easier for them.

The other factor is that once you've done all this, it's embarrassing for them to say they can't decide. It makes it harder for them to back out. Plus their trust in you is built up. Who else would go to all the trouble to drag chairs around the store unless they really wanted to make sure you got the right item? So when you say it's a good idea to buy it, they believe you.

So the keys to this step are just keep asking questions and listen to the answers. The other one is use your wits to make it easy for them to decide between their choices. Get them to figure out what they want!

Chapter Nine

Step Five: When Do They Want It?

After you know exactly what they want, then you need to know when they want it. This is the last piece of information you need in order to make an effective close. To keep control of the sale you want to find out when they want it before you tell them how long it takes. If you tell them how long it takes before you know when they want it, you're giving up control and depending on luck. What can happen is: If it takes three weeks to get and they want it in four, they'll come back in a week to order it. If you tell them it's in stock and they want it in two weeks, they'll come back in two weeks to pick it up. The reason is that most customers truly believe they are the only people buying this item, so it will always be there. In their mind they have no reason to give you a deposit, so they don't. You are not going to be able to explain to them that they aren't the only ones buying this product and there is no guarantee the item is going to be there when they want it, so don't try. Just accept the fact and deal with it.

I've been using tables as an example all along, so I'll continue. Ask, "If you were to get a table, when would you be wanting it?"

The timing on this question is very important in order to get a straight answer. The time to ask is after you know exactly what they want. They're sitting at the table with a faraway look in their eyes imagining it in their house, preferably touching the item. They're relaxed. They just commented how nice it was or something like that.

If you time it right when they are "under the ether," as my friend used to say, they will tell you when they want it. Then go to the close and tailor it to their time needs. If you time it wrong, or say it wrong they will ask, "How long does it take?" The control is now reversed. You have to time it when they are in the heat of desire and say it word for word. Don't say, "When would you want it?" because they can say, "I didn't say I want it." Now you're pushy. Say, "If you were to get a table, when would you be wanting it?"

The best way to handle it when they ask "How long does it take?" is to say, "Let me go check". After you've turned and taken a couple of steps toward your inventory records, say, "When would be a good time for you?" Raise your voice and put the accent on the word "time." Don't say anything else, and keep walking. Almost always the customers will then tell you when they need it. It's the same principal as in the greeting. When you turn away their wall starts to come down. After a few steps, it's all the way down. So you ask them the same question in different words, and they'll usually give you a straight answer. You've regained control!

Now you have the complete picture of their wants and needs. This leads to the close (where you explain to them why they want to give you money today). For example, if they want a particular item at a particular time, they can do that so long as they give you the money that's required. If they say they want it in a couple of weeks and it takes one week to get or you have it in stock, say, "According to our records, we can do that for you if you place an order." Then go on to the close. If they want it before you can get it, then you know to close them and be ready to explain why it's worth the wait. If you have it in stock and they want it now, that's the best!

Never lie to customers, but don't shoot yourself in the foot either by saying what you don't have to. If they ask questions, always answer them honestly. There's just some stuff you don't have to volunteer. If they don't tell you when they want it on the second try, which sometimes happens, just tell them how long it takes and close them knowing you're shooting in the dark. The sample close in the next chapter is an example of a close to use when you don't know when they want it.

Normally by the end of this step you know exactly what they want, when they want it, and the presentation has given them desire for it. Now they're ready to be closed on the deal!

Chapter Ten

Step Six: The Close

The old how to sell books used to say close the customer at least seven times before giving up. Some would say not only to close often but early so you can find out what the customer's objections to buying are. The reason you can close someone seven times without them getting annoyed with you is this. You ask them to buy, and they give you a reason they won't. They say, "I have to measure." Or, "I'm not sure of the color", whatever. You then show them how this is not a problem, they agree, and you close them again. Then they come up with another reason not to buy, you solve that problem, and you close them again.

It goes something like this.

Salesperson: "...so if you're interested, I'll take your name and number and set up a time good for you..."

Customer: "I'm not sure a 42" table will fit."

Salesperson: "What size table do you have in there now?"

Customer: "It's a 36"x60" rectangular table."

Salesperson: "No problem! A round table actually takes up less space than a rectangular table because it's round. The 42" will be smaller than the 60" on the length. On the width, it's only 42" across the middle. The rest of it continues to get smaller from there. And if you put it where you have your table now, it's only going to stick out three inches on either side of what you have now. (show three inches bigger with your fingers spread.) Can you add this much extra on either side of the table you have now?"

Customer: "Oh sure. That's not much bigger at all."

Salesperson: "That's the nice thing about a round table. You can seat more people and take up less space than you can with a rectangular table."

Customer: "That's true."

Salesperson: "So, let's order it!"

Customer: "I'm still not sure of the color."

Salesperson: Is your other furniture in the room closer to this color or this color?"

Customer: "That color."

Salesperson: "Real wood is all different shades on the same item. The natural boards are different colors. All you can do is blend them. You can't match them exactly because the tree doesn't grow that way. But solid wood will last much longer than most other materials."

Customer: "That's true."

Salesperson: " Did you want to pick this up or have it delivered?"

Customer: " I'm not sure of the style."

You get the idea. Yes, you can close people seven times at least without offending them. But you can make the sale a lot calmer by figuring out what the customers want and when they want it before you close them.

If you followed the previous five steps and didn't skip any, you can avoid all this. By the time you get to this step, you should know what your customers want and when they want it. You should have a good rapport with them. They should be looking at you as a friend and an expert on what you sell. They should be reassured by this friend and expert that their choices are good ones. Now all you have to do is close the deal by explaining how to buy it.

Only close when all the parties concerned are there. On furniture or big-ticket items in retail, usually that means the husband and the wife. You close them when they are really desiring it. Then you lull them even deeper in the trance with the close. If you close the wife and then you go look for the husband to explain it to him, you've lost that emotional advantage. The wife might cool off. The husband needs to have his desire for the product built up in him before you can close him.

People aren't logical. You have to acknowledge the emotions. So don't bother to close until all parties are present. It won't work. It's also important that the close is said smoothly without interruption. It's like the presentation, with the rhythmic cadence of your delivery. You're lulling them into doing it, or as my friend used to say, putting them under the ether.

The following is the basic close we used to use.

CLOSE

"If you were to get a table, when would you be wanting it?" ("How long does it take?")."Let me check. When would be a good time for you?" ("It doesn't matter".)

"Right now it takes about two weeks. If that's too fast, we can hold the price for two months. In return for the order, we hold the price, and guarantee you it will be here when you want it. You come out, and if you like it, you can take it with you at this price. You don't like it or change your mind, we give you your deposit back. And the deposit is only ten per cent.

So if you're seriously interested, I'll take your name and number and set up a time that's good for you."

I would have people memorize it cold just like the presentations. It was the close you used when you didn't know when they wanted it. So by memorizing it, the salespeople learned our basic ordering system for stock items. You tried to make as big of a net as possible. Surely they wanted it before two months! If they didn't buy, then your next question is, "Is two months too fast for you?" They'll either say yes or give you their real objection. Then you can try to solve that objection. If you knew when they wanted it, you would adapt the close to the customer's situation. "If you want it in a week, we can do that if you place an order. In return for the order…"

This close worked really well. Instead of saying, "If you want to buy it" or something like that, we would say, "If you're seriously interested". It was much easier wording for them to agree to. If the item was a stock item, we would make the deposit refundable. The thinking was we were going to have it in stock anyway so why not? They rarely cancel if you reaffirm them, which I'll explain later on in this chapter. If it was special order, the deposit was thirty per cent and non-refundable.

Most customers assume all deposits are non-refundable. So the only time you needed to tell them about the refundability of the deposit in the close was when it was a refundable deposit.

The non-refundable deposit close would go like this. ...."You come out and pick it up at this old price. And the deposit is only thirty per cent. So if you're seriously interested, I'll take your name and number and call when it's ready."

As soon as you mention money or deposit, the customer will generally freeze up. An old salesman friend of mine once said that the customer will be real friendly and responsive through the whole sale, but as soon as you start crawling around in his back pocket looking for money, he'll freeze up and get tense. What happens a lot of times when you mention money is that the customers go from listening to you to thinking about money. Upcoming bills, adding up the items they want, their financial situation, whatever. They'll still be looking at you, but he's not listening. Their minds are elsewhere.

This is why you mention the deposit last. You tell all the positive things the order does for them first. Then at the very end you mention money. You take the sting out of it with the refundable deposit. With the non-refundable deposit, you tell all the positive things the order will do, then just say "And the deposit is only thirty per cent!" Enough said. You don't have to make them more tense by telling them the deposit is non-refundable. They already assume that since most deposits normally are. You tell them that it's non-refundable while you're writing up the order and you get to the part in the order about the deposit. You say, "The deposit is thirty per cent, that's non-refundable, and we'll call you as soon as it's here". This is after you've gotten their name, address and exactly what they're ordering written down. Then it's no problem. Make it as smooth as you can.

The danger in a refundable deposit is that a weak sales person will sell the fact that the deposit is refundable, not the features of the item. If you keep telling the customers they have nothing to lose and they can always cancel, they probably will. They do what you say. The refundable deposit is just one more bullet in your arsenal, not the whole ball of wax.

I did a craft show one time and sold on the refundability of the deposit, not the features of the table. I got nine orders and all of them cancelled later. Instead of making it a strong sale, I'd tell them they had nothing to lose by ordering it to push them over. That doesn't work very well! One guy said to me, "You mean if I give you a deposit, you'll quit talking to me? And then I get it back? O.K., I'll do it!" I'm telling you, a lot of this stuff was learned the hard way!

As soon as your customers agree to order, start writing immediately. Remember, buying is an emotional thing, not a logical thing. There have been many times when people have said, "Okay, I'd like to order it. Let me look around at what else you have and then we'll write it up right before I leave." A lot of times after they look around the store, they say, "It's really nice, we'll be back." The reason they do this is their excitement cools down as they look around. The doubts about whether they should buy it come back. Then they're gone.

To avoid this you say, "Okay." Then pause a second and say, "Let me get some information from you while it's still fresh in my mind so I don't forget any thing". They'll say okay and then you start writing and don't look up.

This works for the same reason it works in the greeting. As soon as they say they want to do something you don't want them to, always agree. Say "okay", then pause. Then say it another way. Again when you say "okay", their wall comes down, and that's the time to tell them what to do. They're relaxed. If you don't say "okay" and pause, they'll say, "I said we want to look around." Words and how you use them are extremely important in sales.

Like I said, as soon as you can, start writing and don't look up. While writing, talk in definite terms and repeat the order as you write it. Once the customer has agreed to order it, all his walls are down and you can pretty much tell him what to do in no uncertain terms. Reaffirming the sale is very important. Do it like this.

"Okay, you wanted a 48" table in the gold finish, right?"

"Yes."

"And six of these chairs, right?"

"Yes."

"And you wanted to pick them up on the first of next month, right?"

"Yes".

"Okay, the deposit is one hundred dollars."

After everything is done, look them in the eye and shake their hand. Say, "Thanks a lot, Mr. or Ms. Whomever. We'll see you on the first. Someone will call the day before to confirm the date. And when people come in and ask where you got the table, here's some cards to give them."

After doing this, in their mind they have bought the table and there's no doubt in anyone's mind they're coming back. They have even agreed to give out cards for referrals on a table they don't have yet! If you don't reaffirm the sale at the end like this, you'll have a higher cancellation rate. They won't take it as seriously without this. They do what you do. If you treat it frivolously, so will they. If you act confident and decisive, so will they.

If you can do it comfortably, the Baptist handshake is the best one to seal a deal. That is the one where you shake hands and clasp your free left hand over the two shaking hands. All the while looking the customer dead in the eye with a smile. Touch plays an important part in human communication but in the U.S. culture we don't really acknowledge that. If you're not comfortable doing it, don't. The customer will pick up on your unease and become nervous also. You want the customer calm and assured. Don't do things to add to his nervousness.

The other way to avoid cancellations is to confirm people's appointment the night before. Just call them and say you were calling to confirm that tomorrow was still a good time for them to come out to pick it up. They either say yes or you change it to another time, which you confirm with them the day before again. Tell them it's so you can have everything in order and the paperwork ready for them. Otherwise they don't take it seriously and figure it will always be there for them to pick up at anytime. And you run out of room in your store room. It'll be filled with stuff having sold tags dangling from them.

Once customers don't show, it's hard to get them to come pick their merchandise up. They realize nothing bad happened to them because they didn't. So they'll pick it up whenever it's convenient to them. Meanwhile you're not getting commission on the stuff piling up in the store room.

So always try to give a friendly reminder call the day before. Be polite, brief, and assume they are coming when they said. Don't be wishy washy and say is it still all right for you to come out or something like that. Don't make it easy to back out or make it seem like everyone changes their pick up date. It's the same attitude you have in the selling process. Assume the sale!

So there you have it. Don't close them until you know what they want and when they want it. Once they order it, keep track of the order until they take it with them.

You now know the six steps of a retail sale. When you start doing it this way, your closing rate will go way up!

Chapter Eleven

Reviewing the Sale

You can't sell everyone but you can sell almost everyone. If someone leaves without buying, review the sale in your mind and see if there was something you could have done to make the sale. The same situation will present itself again. You can count on that. Some occur more often than others do, but the same situation will reoccur. Selling is a day by day profession, just like sports. It doesn't matter what you did yesterday, it's today's game that counts. It's not like some jobs that you can do while half asleep and nobody notices the difference. So like sports, even though you've been doing it for years, you have to practice and constantly analyze what you did right or wrong. Be honest with yourself in your appraisal of what happened. The purpose is for you to sell as many people as possible. The only way that is going to happen is if you're honest with yourself or whoever is helping you review the sale. Don't let ego get in the way of your success. You're not there to look good or feel superior. You're there to sell as much as you can.

Not everything is in your control. The three main legitimate reasons for people not buying is you don't have what they're looking for, they don't have the money, or they have to bring back a spouse or other partner in the sale.

If you don't have exactly what they want, you may have something that's just as good. You have to use your wits and be creative. Think of a new use for something that you normally associate with another function. I sold a china hutch to a man looking for a combination bookcase entertainment center. We had entertainment centers, but he liked the hutch better. So I let him get it. He thanked me profusely.

If customers don't have the money and they don't qualify for financing, credit cards, lay away, etc., the only way you can make that sale is if you yourself lend them the money. I advise you don't do that. Just let them go until they come up with the money later on their own.

As I said before only close when all decision making parties are there. If they have to bring someone back, let them. Just get them all excited about it so they do bring the other person back. From trial and error I know that's the best way to get the sale. When we first started, I was the only salesperson in the store. I knew who came back and who didn't. If I closed a wife or husband on the fact that the deposit was refundable so if the other spouse didn't like it they got their deposit back, they would usually almost always cancel. If I browbeat them to order it and they didn't order it but said they'd "be back", they wouldn't be back. If I got them excited but didn't close them, they would usually come back and buy. You can keep track of these things better if you're the only one working the store.

Bill the used car salesman was amazed at the be-backs he had. In used cars be-backs didn't exist. You either sold them now or you never saw them again. He found that during the days of the week, he would see a lot of wives come in to shop the store without their husbands. Everybody knew they couldn't buy anything without their husbands so most salespeople in most stores ignored them and let them look. Bill found that by giving them a lot of attention and following all the steps except the close he would stand out in the wives' minds compared to the other stores and other salespeople. He was amazed because they actually did bring their husbands back on the weekend like they said they would and usually would buy.

One time we had someone die before his order came in. There isn't anything you can do about that either. The rest of the reasons I'm going to tell you are not valid, even though you hear them all the time. Because of ego, salespeople use many excuses as to why the sale couldn't be made. Smart salespeople try to figure out how to avoid these problems in the future so they can pay their bills.

The nice thing about using the six steps is that they will help you make a sale if you follow them. They will also help you learn why you didn't make a particular sale. When I was teaching people how to sell, I realized that all I did was go down the steps with the salesperson after each sale they didn't make. That was how we found out what needed to be fixed in the salesperson's approach and method.

Salespeople would come to me and say, "I didn't make that sale". I'd go down each step and ask the following questions at each one.

Step One: The Greeting
   "What did they want?"
Step Two: The Presentation
   "Did you give them the presentation?"
Step Three: "How long have you been looking?
   "How long had they been looking?"
Step Four: What exactly do they want?
   "What exactly did they want"
Step Five: When do they want it?
   "When did they want it?"
Step Six: The Close
   "Did you close them?"

If the salesperson answered "No" or "I don't know" to any of these questions, well that was where the problem was. So now they knew where they needed to improve.

We would keep these six steps posted in the lunchroom. That way the salesperson could review his own sale by just looking at each step and asking himself the questions I would ask them. It makes it a lot easier to learn the skill of selling.

The following are six common excuses that salespeople give for their customers not buying. I know you've heard them before too. If you really study them, you will find they aren't valid.

Reason One

"They were just looking". If they say they are just looking and never tell you what they are looking for, you're doing the greeting wrong. Maybe it's where you're standing. Maybe too many salespeople are congregated up front. Maybe you didn't accent the "Yes sir?" right. Maybe you didn't let them stop before you greeted them. Maybe you let them stop twice before you greeted them. Maybe you didn't say "Oh, okay", before you asked them the second time what they were looking for. You'll usually find the reason this happened. Try not to make the same mistake again!

Reason Two

"They had a lot of reasons they didn't like our item". Did you give them the presentation? That's what the presentation does. It answers objections before they come up and builds desire for the product. If you're getting a lot of objections to something, then either the presentation doesn't address these objections up front, or you didn't even give it.

One time a man and a woman came in a van a little before closing time. He said he'd been looking all day for an oak pedestal table. As soon as I showed ours to him, he said, "That's it. Do you have it in stock? I've got a van, I want to take it now." I said yes, we had two and he could take whichever one he wanted.

As soon as he started picking one out, for the first time the woman started talking. It turned out she was his sister. She said, "Don't these tables wobble?" He stopped looking. I told them about the adjustable legs. Then she said, "Don't they warp and crack?" I told her about the finish underneath. Then she wanted to know if the wood was fragile and if it would get water rings and burn and dent. I told her about the hard wood and how you could refinish it, etc., but I was on the defensive and not in control. She got the brother to have doubts and they left with out buying. It seemed like such a sure thing that I never gave the presentation. I went straight for the close, and I lost it. After that I always gave the presentation if they hadn't heard it before, even if they said they wanted to buy it right out. I'd say, "Okay, let me show you how it's made because it is a little different from most and you should know that." Then boom, no more objections.

The best way to handle problems is to avoid them. We never had objections to wobbly tables or cracked wood as long as we gave the presentation. So when this happens, you probably didn't give the presentation right, or your presentation is not handling an objection up front. You may also have given the presentation to only one person in a two person buying unit.

The main point is, your presentation should answer your most common objections up front and be easy to understand.

Reason Three

They liked it. They picked out what they wanted to get. They told me when they wanted it. They wanted to look around more and left. I'd hear that a lot from the people who worked for me. I'd ask the salesperson how long they had been looking. They forgot to ask. It sounds like this is probably the first place they've looked, and they want to satisfy themselves that this really does compare favorably with other stuff.

If they just started looking and it's something you can use a refundable close on, you tailor that close to their situation. You say, "The order will guarantee the price and guarantee it will be here when you want it. If you look around in the meantime and find something you like better, we give you back your deposit. Although frankly, the more people look around, the more they like this. So if you're seriously interested, which you seem to be. I'll take your name and number and set up a good time for you."

You're not asking them to buy it, but if they're interested, you'll write up an order. By saying, "which you seem to be" worked really well on people who were very indecisive. The customers say, "Yes, I'm interested", then you can go write it up in the definite, assume the sale terms I described in the close chapter. Usually, if they look around at all, it's only one other place. And that place doesn't give a presentation, so yours looks better. Then the customers don't bother looking anymore.

Reason Four

"They had to go home and measure."
"They weren't sure which size they wanted".
"They couldn't decide between the two chairs."

You didn't find out what exactly they wanted. You can't sell them until you know this. Figure out what you could have done to make it easy for them to decide. Each one is different. You'll have to use your wits and the wits of the people you work with to figure out what you could have done in that particular situation. Maybe the answer is to put two items next to each other. Maybe the answer is in the words you used.

Reason Five

"They liked everything. They wanted to look around more". Did you ask them when they wanted it?

The weirdest one I had where this was the case went like this. I did everything except asking him when he wanted it. I kept closing him to buy one now. He would say, "Let me think about it" and then just stare at the table. I knew he wanted it, but this went on for an uncomfortable half an hour. Finally, he asked to go outside and smoke a cigarette. I went out to smoke too, and he asked me if he could order it for later as he really didn't have the money but would later on. I felt like an idiot. However, now that I knew when he wanted it, I explained our order system and we set up a time that was good for him to pick it up. You have to know when they want it so that you know how to close them.

Reason Six

They left without buying. They liked it and you did all the steps except you forgot to ask them to buy it. Don't laugh. I've seen this happen a lot. Especially with new sales people who are afraid to ask them to buy.

You've got to ask them to buy it after you've gone through everything else. It's very rare that the customer will volunteer to buy without you asking.

Conclusion

So, as you can see, none of these are legitimate reasons. They're all under your control. They're not good reasons like no money or death or something that is out of your control. Remember that this is not an ego thing. Don't be embarrassed or too proud to admit a mistake. You have to be open minded if you're going to sell most of the people you talk to.

I used to review sales people on their last missed sale, just going down the steps. If there was a legitimate reason for them not buying, fine. If it was something the salesman did, fine. Everyone makes mistakes. That's no big deal. The trick is to try to learn from them. That's the mark of a secure person with a good perspective.

Anyone who acts as though they never make mistakes and it's never their fault is telling you they're insecure with themselves. Relax, we're all human. Don't worry about it. Everyone knows everyone makes mistakes. But not everyone tries to learn from them! By reviewing your sales against the six steps, you are ever increasing your odds for success in future sales.

PART THREE

SPECIFIC SITUATIONS

Chapter Twelve
How to Handle Be-Backs

Some people who didn't buy the first time they're in really do come back like they say they will. Most people don't come back like they say they will. For God's sake don't count on them coming back. You'll starve!

A friend of mine did a craft show next to a minister selling paintings. All the people that came up to the minister's paintings said they would come back and buy one or the other painting before the show was over. He would actually add up in his head the sales he was due to get anytime now. By the end of the show he was devastated. No one had come back to buy. Instead of having a show where he sold nothing, in his own mind he lost all the money which he had calculated he was going to make. So psychologically, he was in even worse shape!

If people come back and say they have been in before, or you recognize them, say, "What did you decide?" They will either tell you what they want to buy, or tell you their problem that needs solved before they can buy. It's a real quick and easy way to cut to the chase. Either they say, "I want to buy this, this and this", or they say, "I still can't decide on size" or color or whatever. Then it's up to you to make it easy for them to decide. Once they do, you have a sale.

I learned this a long time ago. A person came in and said, "See, I told you I'd be back!" I couldn't remember him, and like a fool I said so. He said, "You remember, I couldn't decide between a 42" table and a 48" table." He replayed the sale for me and went over his dilemma at that time. While he was describing it, he got confused again about the size and left. Another salesperson was watching this debacle and commented, "What does it matter if you remember him or not? Just automatically ask, 'What did you decide?' and get on with it!" Duh!

If the customer is bringing back the spouse, there are several ways this can go. You want to give the presentation to the person who hasn't had one. But you want to say the same thing in slightly different wording so it doesn't sound exactly the same to the person that's already heard it. All presentations must sound like a spontaneous regular part of the conversation to be effective. Just say to the one whom is seeing it for the first time, "Let me show you how it's made."

If it's the woman bringing back the guy, your odds are really good for making the sale. Give the presentation, but let the wife sell him if she can. She'll be much better at it than you because she knows him better. If she's smart, she'll bring him in and show him the entire store before she shows him the item she really wants. She'll tell you in the greeting what they're looking for and tell you she wants to show him the store first. Let her. Keep an eye on them, but don't hang around.

This is the best be-back situation. One, it's the woman bringing back the man. Two, if the man is grumpy about buying, when they first come in is when his defensive walls are the highest. He's all set to nix the deal no matter what you say or do. By leading him around the whole store first, these walls get worn down.

He'll nix the first few things she shows him, and she won't mind because she doesn't really want them now anyway. Once he gets this negative stuff out of his system and exhaustion starts to set in, that's when she takes him to what she really wants. It's much easier then. The same principles apply to anyone bringing back a more reluctant partner.

When they get to the item they want, then walk over. Usually she'll ask you to tell him how it's made. Even if they don't specifically ask you to do this, give them the presentation anyway. It's better if you change the words and delivery slightly so it doesn't sound canned to her, since she's heard it once before. The presentation should sound like part of a normal conversation, not a canned pitch like a lot of telemarketers do.

If the guy is bringing the wife back, it's normally a little harder. Again, you can't predict what everyone will do, but you can predict what most will do. Usually he brings her to what he wants first, when her walls are the highest. Even if she likes it, she normally won't want to buy it because, in furniture anyway, she wants to decide on what goes in the house. If she says yes, this is great, she runs the risk that after a while, he'll just start bringing stuff home without her even being in on it. She doesn't want that, so she'll make it a little hard on him. That way he'll always consult her first. Don't try to fight or deny this truism. Just accept it and deal with it.

If this happens, you'll probably have to come up with an item that's slightly different. Just show her all your attention, and find out what she wants. Treat her with great respect and ask lots of questions about what exactly she's looking for. Don't worry too much about whoever is bringing the other one back, as they're pretty much sold anyway.

The main things for you to remember are don't count on be-backs; and if you do luck out and get one, just cut to the chase and ask, "What did you decide?"

Chapter Thirteen
How to Handle Order Pickups

The six steps will get the sale closed. Now you need to get the customer to take it away happily and paid in full. If you do it right, not only will you have that sale, but if the entire experience was good you'll eventually get referrals and repeat business. Sales on people that are referrals and repeats are much easier than someone coming in off an ad.

It depends on what you're selling as to how much attention you give to your product. In furniture it's good to check over the item before the customer comes to get it. Remember that the best way to handle problems is to avoid them. If it's something you have a lot of in stock, you don't have to worry too much about it. You can always get another one. If it's a special order and you have to wait eight weeks to get another one, you want to be more careful.

The best people to pre-check the item are salespeople. They know what the customer is expecting, and they hear the complaints about the product. So they know what to look for. Don't assume that it'll be perfect when it comes out of the box. What's acceptable to a manufacturer or a warehouseman is not always acceptable to customers who are paying good money to put something in their house. Also, the customers usually don't have that much knowledge about furniture, but there are certain things they usually pay attention to. There's a real difference in perspective here. We used a checklist that was based on previous customer complaints. We checked that the finish was smooth and the drawers opened easily. We checked for cracks, missing hardware, anything that a customer complained to us about in the past.

When customers come out to pick their purchase up, just bring it out and say, "Here it is." Don't tell them to look it over. The key is having a confident, proud air about you. If you're hesitant and nervous about them looking at it, they are going to want to study it to see what you're nervous about. They will follow your lead, as always.

Ask them what kind of car they have next, so you get an idea of how to load it. It gets their mind on that and not on looking to see what's wrong with it. Since you checked it before they got there, you should have a confident air about you. If there's nothing obviously wrong, you're good to go. I used to tell people "If you think it looks good here, wait until you see it in a home setting. They look much nicer in a home setting than in a warehouse setting". This gets them imagining it in their home. And it's true. We'd have people call and say, "This looks unbelievable in our house." That's a great ending. Now they're higher on the item than ever before. This is good for referrals and repeat business.

That's the other thing to remember, keep your perspective. Realize you're looking for something wrong in an unflattering situation when you check it over. When it's in a home being used, that setting will make it look much better. Also, people will be using it, not studying it for flaws. The piece will look great.

We had a guy who made custom furniture for important members of the U.S. government picking up some chairs one time. People that made or knew furniture were easy to sell because they knew our stuff was a good deal. He was picking up his chairs next to a guy who was picking up a table. The table guy was studying every detail. The furniture maker saw this and said, "What are you doing, looking for flaws?" The other man nodded yes. The furniture maker said, "Why bother? They all disappear once they're in the house anyway!" The other man got embarrassed and stopped looking.

I thought that was a great line. It's true! When people don't know much if anything about the item you're selling, and they start looking for flaws, you've got a problem. They don't know what they're looking at or for. They get real insecure and scared. They just keep studying it, working themselves into a panic. For God's sakes, don't do this to them. It's very cruel.

The danger in not checking the item first is that if the customer sees something obviously wrong, like a drawer sticking or a crack in the wood, then their trust in you is shot! Now they want to see what other mistakes were made on it. Nothing is perfect. If you study anything long enough, you will find something wrong with it. Now you're in a downward spiral that is very difficult to come out of.

Don't give the customer a reason to tell his friends how he went to pick it up and had to have it fixed or reordered or all of that. Then, if by chance you do get a referral or repeat business from him, their guard will be up. They'll be looking hard for something wrong.

And they will probably find it. Earn that trust and avoid problems. There are enough problems without you adding to them!

If the customer sees something wrong and asks to have it fixed, and you can fix it, say, "Sure, no problem. Is this the one you want?" If they say they're not sure yet, then say, "No problem. If you decide you want it, I'll take care of that for you."

So only fix it if they say they definitely want it if the repair is satisfactory. The reason is if you fix it right away, without them saying they definitely want it, then it's almost as if they enjoy watching you fix things. So they just keep looking for more and more. When you're finally done, they usually don't want it because it's all patched up. What a waste of time for you. I've done it both ways, and the first way is the best. Of course the very best way is check it yourself first so you don't have to deal with any of it.

No matter how well the customer is treated, it's the last impression he remembers most. So loading the car is very important to future sales. We had a guy loading cars for us who would be upset if he didn't make at least ten dollars in tips for a three-hour shift in the early evening. It was that routine for him. No one else ever got tips like he did. So I asked him what he did and said.

He would shake hands with the customer and introduce himself. He would say that it was a nice piece the customer had just bought. Then he would ask to see the car and tell the customer how he was going to put it in the car. Some items would get tied to the top, others would go in the trunk. Then he would calmly, quickly, and carefully put it in the car. If it took a while to do, and he talked to the customer while doing it, the conversation would be about the customer. He made the customer the star. At the end most would be so appreciative, they would tip him.

The other people loading cars had loaded thousands of cars and acted like it. They usually didn't say anything, they just put it in the car. If they did talk, it was about everybody's favorite subject, themselves. Sometimes the customers would worry about how they were going to put it in the car and give suggestions. This would cause unease and distrust between the loader and the customer. Since the other guy had explained in advance in a confident way how he was going to load the car, this never happened to him. He had avoided that problem. And getting tips from a satisfied customer rarely happened to the other loaders!

So there you have the complete sales process. Remember the last thing they see is the thing they remember most. So make the entire pick up process pleasant, smooth and professional.

Chapter Fourteen
How to Deal With Competition

It's better for you not to have competition. If you do have other stores selling the same or similar items, this chapter will show you how to handle them.

When we first opened a second store, an old customer from our first store stopped by to look around. While he was there, he took it upon himself to tell the salespeople there why he shopped at our store. He said he knew he would be treated with respect. He had a problem with a rocker he bought from us and we gave him a replacement. No problem, no questions asked. So he knew we would be there for him after the sale. He knew our quality was good. So now, he doesn't shop around. If he needs a particular item in furniture, he goes to us first. If we have it, he buys it. He may have been able to find it a little cheaper with some serious looking. But he wouldn't have had the respect and the after-sale service. The lower price wasn't worth it. He knew he could trust us. That was what was the most important thing.

Retail people frequently think price is the most important thing in the sale. That's why some stores have permanent "Sale" signs in their windows. I've found that's not true. Price and quality are important, but the main thing customers seem to go for is being treated right. When something is wrong and it bothers them to the point that they call you or bring it back, take care of it for them. It will make you more money in the long run. If you don't take care of it, not only will they not shop there anymore, they'll tell their friends not to go to you either.

If you give customers a hassle when they bring something back, it means that it happens so often that you would go broke taking care of all the complaints. That's not a good message. I used to have people come up to me while I was selling someone. They would say, "This stuff is great. I bought a table from them. It cracked and they gave me a new one." That used to bother me. It didn't seem like much of an endorsement. But to them it was. It meant you could trust us to be there for you. And that was more important to them than price or quality. That's obvious, since that was what they mentioned!

Always check out your competition's store so you know what you're up against. Customers will come in, and some will exaggerate how great your competitor's store is so that your confidence will go down and you'll be more likely to cut a deal. Knowledge is strength. The main rule on competition is never to knock the competition to the customer. Even if what you say is true and the customer knows it to be true, it won't work. The customer will see you as a mean spirited, gossipy, petty person. His sympathy will go to the competitor, not you. The only thing you can do is sell your product the best you can and not mention the competition. If the customer brings up your competitor, just say, " I've been there, it's nice," and go on with the sale. The more time you spend discussing the competition, the less time you talk about your own products. Every time the competition is mentioned (positively or negatively), it is free advertising for your competitor!

If customers ask which is better, you or your competitor, say, "I think we have the best value, but that's up to you to decide. Usually they are surprised you didn't trash the competition and impressed with your fairness. Most people prefer to deal with nice people. In fact, hope that your competition knocks you. It makes them look petty and worried about you. People then come over to your store to see what he was talking about.

We used to have a competitor who has since gone out of business. Part of their standard sales pitch was to say theirs was a better deal than ours. We had people that were going to buy from them come over and buy from us. More than once we heard, "When we went over to buy a table at your competitors, they kept talking about you. We had never heard of you before, but figured you must have similar furniture. So we came over to see what you had." Thanks a lot!

That's how I learned knocking the competition is not a good idea, even if what you're saying is true. Just do your best and let the customers decide whom they would rather deal with. Hopefully when they compare you with them, you'll look more professional, knowledgeable, secure, and have much better quality. The competitor will look insecure, paranoid about competition and too eager to make a deal strictly on price and not what the product will do for the customers. If you give a presentation on the facts and benefits of your product and they don't, you'll be the one that customers assume has the quality product. Especially if your competitor is hung up on price.

When the competitor I mentioned earlier did go out of business, we got all of their customers who didn't get the furniture they ordered. There seemed to be two types of customers they sold. One type was the kind that had money and just wanted furniture and were going to buy it from whoever had what they were looking for first. They really didn't care where that was or how much it cost. They just wanted to get it and go on with life.

The second type were really hardcore dealers. They had just lost hundreds of dollars in deposits with the competitor. But they still wanted to deal. The store knew they were going out of business in a few months. So they were making outrageous deals to people. Free delivery, thirty per cent off if you paid in full for your deposit, etc. Why not? They knew they weren't going to have to sell it to them for that price anyway since they were going to be gone.

I had one guy who was crying about losing his five hundred dollar deposit at that store. When he picked out what he wanted, he said the other place gave him twenty per cent off and asked if I would do the same. I told him the other place gave it to him because they knew they were going out of business and he wasn't going to get it anyway, so they knew it didn't matter what they said. But we planned to be in business and actually deliver the goods to him and that was why we couldn't give him the discount. He walked out anyway. That's hard core.

All the other types of customers didn't seem to buy there. Just the easy sales, lay downs as they're called and the hard core bargainers. That wasn't enough of a customer base to keep them in business.

Another way we kept competition troubles down to a minimum was having two types of oak pedestal tables. The one we mainly sold was built with much thicker wood. The competition sold one made of thinner wood but the same style. It was a little bit cheaper. The customer couldn't really remember the difference. They both looked the same in his memory. It was just that the other was cheaper. We started carrying a thinner version also that was cheaper than the thicker. We wouldn't knock the competition, we would just explain the difference between the two. Our thinner one was the same price as everyone else's. Some people liked the looks or price of the thinner one and bought it anyway. That was one sale we got that the competition didn't.

Most people preferred the thicker one that cost a little more. We got a name for quality. And the closing rate was up because people didn't have to go back to the other stores to compare again. They could make their decision at our store. If your customer is writing down prices and such, try to get him to quit. But don't tell him to quit. Say, "What you'll find is our prices are good. But the main difference we have here is the quality. Like this." Then proceed to point out more features and benefits. Usually they'll quit writing and go back to listening to you. Most people only take notes on prices and sizes, not quality.

If you've ever gone to a bunch of stores and wrote down the item and the price, when you get home, all you have is pages of numbers. You can't remember what the item even looked like. But if you were told at one store that the quality was the main point, you'll remember that, especially if everyone else is selling price. You can't be different if you're just like everyone else!

If the customer doesn't seem sold on your product after the presentation, and it doesn't make any sense, ask, "How does this compare with what you've been looking at?" They will either say it compares better than what they've been looking at or not. If it compares better, the more they talk about how much better yours is, the more they're selling themselves. This is great. They'll sell themselves much better than you ever could. If they say they've seen something they like better and describe it to you, then you know what you're up against. Now that you know, it's up to you to use your wits to figure out what you have available that they will like better than what they saw elsewhere. The key to sales is asking questions. If you can't figure something out about the customer, ask!

If people come in and says they can get the same thing down the street for a lesser price, then you know right away it's not true. If it were then why are they at your store telling you? Why aren't they buying it down the street? There must be a difference. The customers would not want to waste their time telling you the news. Either yours is better, or if it is the same, maybe you can get it quicker. Don't be intimidated. Just keep selling your product. If necessary, call the other store and pretend you're a customer and ask about the particular item. There is always some reason the customer is at your store and not the place that has the same thing cheaper!

We found that in this case, sometimes it was the same item, but the other store's item was reduced because of damage. Or it took a long time to get and ours was in stock. Or it was a cheap imitation. The customers know that. That's why they are at your store instead. Don't accuse him of knowing this already. Always be nice and helpful!

So, know what your competition has, but never knock your competition. Try to have a wide selection so customers can make their decision right there. Put on your best professional, trustworthy show and let the customer decide whom he would rather give his money to. If you do it right, most times that store will be yours.

Chapter Fifteen

Communicating To Different Customers

Communication by talking means to talk in such a way that the other person understands what you're saying. Otherwise you're wasting your time. The purpose is to get your idea across, not try to impress them with your knowledge of big words and technical jargon. Keep it simple!

If your customers are slow talking and acting, you need to slow down to their level. If they're fast and into just the facts, you need to be the same. You want to communicate on an equal level. Don't talk fast and crisp if they're very slow. Don't talk really slow if they're fast and crisp. You'll probably get on their nerves.

A great salesman was on his home phone talking to a customer. His wife was listening to his side of the conversation. When he hung up she asked, "Whom were you talking to? That didn't even sound like you." He was from Brooklyn and the customer was from Minnesota. So he was talking much slower than usual. This was so he could get his message across. Like I said, he was a top salesman.

We had a woman work for us who at the end of the day said she felt like she had been twenty different personalities. Again, she was adapting to the customer so the customer could understand her. You always want to be yourself, but be sensitive enough to the customers to speak to them in a way that they understand. You don't want to fake an accent, just be aware of whom you're talking to. Any extrovert and someone known for getting along with people does this naturally. The woman at work who said she felt like she had been twenty different people, did that naturally. It was just that in the store she talked to a lot more people than she usually did in the course of a day.

Find out what the customers are into and go accordingly. Some people are into the way it's made. Stress the structure. Some people are into looks. Stress the looks. Adapt to the customers. Don't try to make the customers adapt to you. Make them feel comfortable. Don't insult them by putting on a fake accent that's similar to theirs. Just relate to them in the same way that they do. If they're shy, you act shy. Still talk to them and control the situation, just do it in a gentle way. If they're bold and not shy, don't be too meek.

These are things people who are people persons do naturally. They can read the body language of a person and know if what they're saying is good or bad. They make adjustments based on this. I've seen people talking where one is making the other one angry. The one talking is oblivious to body language and is totally surprised when the other person blows up. Some people have this gift naturally. Others have to be taught. They need to read a book on body language or Dale Carnegie's book, *How To Win Friends And Influence People.* But I'm not going to get into that here. That's already been done.

All I can say is that people are mirrors of you. You be friendly, decisive, and upbeat; the people you're talking to will probably be too. If you're sad, unfriendly, or scared to talk, the other person probably will be, too.

If people come in grumpy because of the oppressive heat, something happening in their life, etc. be aware that you can mirror them. You're a person too. Then you may end up grumpy or surly for the rest of the day. Then you can bet all of the customers you talk to will be grumpy. Keep your perspective, and don't let yourself be affected by a grumpy customer. You do that and you've set the tone for the rest of the day. You control them, don't let them control you and your day!

Keep your language simple so any one can understand. We've all read that newspapers are written on a grade school reading level. I read a how to sell book that said after the salesman wrote a presentation, he would give it to a twelve year old. If the twelve-year-old couldn't understand it, he would rewrite it and try it again. It does no good to talk to people if they don't understand what you're saying.

You also have to talk in a way so that people are listening by raising and lowering your voice, etc. You talk to a young couple in a different way than you do an old couple. That seems obvious to me. One thing I learned is that the younger the salespeople are the more serious they should be. The older the salespeople are, the more energetic they should be. This is the "give them what they don't expect rule." They see an old salesperson coming toward them, they're expecting slow and out of touch. They see a young salesperson coming toward them, they expect giddy and inexperienced in life. Give them what they don't expect.

If you're obviously foreign in appearance, but you speak perfect English, people are thrown off. Any time you throw them off, they're easier to control. If your store is dumpy on the outside, make sure inside is very organized and neat. That is not what they're expecting, and they get curious. They listen to you.

Those are basic rules on salesmanship. Like I said, there are many books written on how to talk to people. The Dale Carnegie book is one. You either do these things naturally, or you have to learn it. Either way, you can do it. The main rule is to remember that people are mirrors of you. If you are upbeat, positive, and decisive, your customers will reflect this.

Chapter Sixteen
How to Handle Advisers

The most potentially frustrating customer combinations are when the customer brings an adviser. This is a friend, relative or acquaintance whose opinion they trust about your product. It's easy to handle, though. Just sell the adviser.

In any group of two or more, you must figure out which one is the decision maker. If there is an adviser in the group, the adviser is the one making the decision. Show that person great respect. When you get to the, "what exactly do they want?" step, let the adviser convince the customer which one to buy.

It's confusing the first time you encounter this. The customer wants one thing. The adviser tells them to get another thing. They argue about it. You figure the customer is over twenty-one, it's a free country, it's his money, so you sell him. It doesn't work that way.

We had a guy looking for a table to go with antique maple chairs. He brought a woman friend to help him decide. She liked an expensive maple table. He liked an inexpensive oak table. The maple table matched the chairs better, but he liked the oak one better. They argued for some time with me listening. Finally I asked him, "Are you married?"

"No."

"Are you living together?"

"No."

"Are you going out together?"

"No."

"Then what does it matter what she wants? Get what you want!"

It made sense to me, but he ended up getting the maple table, the whole time saying he'd rather get the oak one. I've seen the same basic scenario with people bringing their mothers in, neighbors, furniture experts etc. That's how I learned you had to sell the adviser.

The person who finally explained to me what was going on was a woman salesperson who worked for us. I was telling her that it didn't make sense to me that some people didn't get what they wanted. She said she used to have a friend bring her to advise her on which clothes to buy, and she did the same thing. She would make the friend get what she thought she should get. She didn't care what the friend wanted. She said to me, "Think about it. What kind of person brings an adviser? It's someone who can't make decisions. They have no faith in themselves. That's why they bring the adviser. They trust them more than they do themselves. So they will always end up getting whatever the adviser says." That made sense to me.

So don't be fooled. When someone comes in with an adviser, sell the adviser what the adviser wants. The adviser will sell the customer, almost every time.

Chapter Seventeen
Sundry Sales Tips

This chapter will consist of various ways to handle certain situations and avoid others.

If the customers are getting serious and want to know the total price of the items they're looking at, include everything in it, the tax, delivery, etc. You'll notice quite a difference in their reaction when you do this. You give them the price, and they automatically ask what the tax and delivery costs are. People are so used to being given base prices that don't include tax and delivery, that no matter what price you give them, they are automatically prepared to add more to it. When they don't have to add anything to it, it seems to be a better value. This is because as soon as you mention the price, they expect it to be more. So it's not as much as they thought it was. Plus they respect and like you more for being up front with them about the total cost.

Lots of stores have sales and make deals. We found it better not to do that if you rely on repeat business. It's best to price your merchandise as low as you need to and still sell it and make money. We found sales made people reluctant to buy until something was on sale. So when there wasn't a sale, it was hard to close them. When you explain that you try to keep your prices as low as possible all the time, rather than raise them and then lower them for a sale, you can close them then and now. They know that by not ordering now, the only change in price that might occur is up in response to inflation. They also respect you more for respecting their intelligence. Customers know the usual scam of sales. Either the price is raised ridiculously and then lowered during a sale to the price it should be, or people just automatically leave "Sale" signs on items 365 days out of the year. The Saturn car company was the first auto manufacturer to recognize this fact. The price on the car is the price. Customers really appreciate that straightforwardness. They don't have to worry that they could have gotten a better price if they had only bargained harder. It takes a lot of stress off the customers. Remember, the more relaxed the customers are, the more likely they'll make a decision.

When customers asked if we could make a deal and lower the price on a set or something, we wouldn't. But we wouldn't say no. We would say, "Most of our business is referrals and repeat customers. To do that we keep our prices as low as we can all the time. That way it's fair for everybody. A lot of places raise their prices and then come down to this price. We found doing it this way people don't get angry because they find out their friend paid less for the same item. It's not fair otherwise!"

That's called taking away their right to self righteousness. Instead of you being the bad guy and saying no, the customer would be the bad guy by getting something cheaper than everyone else. You don't lower your price, and you create no hard feelings. In the early days we would sometimes try to give people a better deal. What happens is as soon as you do that, you go from being their friend to the enemy. They got that out of you, now they want to see what else they can get out of you. The only way to get it to stop is to be mean and say no more. It's much more pleasant and you have much better sales figures if you don't have special sales events. Remember that price and quality are important, but how people are treated in your store is the most important thing.

Don't tell jokes to the customer. What you think is funny he may not. It's bad when that happens. Don't talk politics, etc. Stay professional and maneuver the sale. One time someone brought up the IRS at the store. I watched the salesman go into a diatribe about how they were bloodsuckers who would jail their own mothers for back taxes. You guessed it. The customer he was talking to worked for the IRS. It wasn't pretty after that. If the customers want to joke or talk about politics, though let them. Make them feel at ease, but keep the flow eventually going to a sale.

If the phone is ringing while you are in the middle of a sale and you are the only one to answer it, then answer it. It is the lesser of two evils. It is usually not good to have the sale interrupted, but if the customer sees you ignoring the phone to sell them, they're going to think that the sale is all you care about. This will erase the trust they have in you and make them much less likely to buy than the interruption will. Plus a constantly ignored ringing phone connotes disorganization, which makes people less likely to trust you to handle their money and order in an organized fashion.

If customers say they need to go home to measure or check something, ask if anyone is home. Then say, "You can use our phone to call and ask. It will save you a trip". You can also pretend to be a customer and call other stores to verify a price, whether they have an item in stock, whatever it takes for them to make a decision in your store now. Notice on that one I said you call the other store. If they call, they may get it wrong or tell you something that's not true. But always do it in a way that it's a favor to the customer. It saves them a trip, it doesn't help you make the sale (even though it does). Every thing you do is for the customers, not you!

Sometimes the reason an item isn't selling is because of where it's positioned. When I first hired the used car salesman, I told him that everyone usually got a particular style of Windsor side chair. I told him everyone liked them because they were comfortable, strong and looked good. Of course, the first week he was there, all the customers complained how uncomfortable they were. No salesperson on our staff could sell them. His trust in my knowledge was seriously challenged!

What happened? I finally realized that the chairs had been switched around on the show room floor. We had all the different chairs lined up in a row. The armchair was the first in line, and the side chair was second. So when the customer tried that style, he sat in the armchair first. That was comfortable. Then he sat in the side chair, and that wasn't nearly as comfortable. Then you ran into problems because the customer wanted all armchairs. But they cost a lot more than the side chair, and they took up a lot more room. Normally they would get one or two armchairs and the rest side chairs. Now they weren't buying any chairs at all. The used car salesman was looking at me like I was crazy for telling him these chairs were easy to sell. Once I realized what had happened, I switched the order back so the side chair was the first thing they sat on. Then they liked the side chair. When they sat on the armchair they really liked that. But now they had also said the side chair was comfortable. So mixing them was not a problem. When I told him what was happening and he saw that the new order worked, his eyes lit up and he said, "Mess with their minds! I love it!" So sometimes it's where you have your items positioned that's hurting sales, not what you're saying or doing.

The other thing that worked well selling chairs that can perhaps be applied to your situation is this. We would give the presentation on the chairs and then say, "And it's a heavy wood." We would then hand the customer the chair by holding two fingers under the top of the chair. The customer would do what we did. Instead of grabbing it with two hands, he would put his two fingers underneath it, too. When we let go, we would just pull our fingers out and let it sink on his fingers. This action made it seem real heavy and they would be impressed. They do what you do. If we handed it to them with two hands and said it was heavy, they would take it with two hands and say, "It's not that heavy." Try it and you'll be amazed. This is the same principal as touching the product with loving respect. They do it too.

Also get into the habit of nodding your head yes periodically while talking. Not all the time but once in a while when your making a good point. They will do it too. It puts them in the yes state of mind. This is a good state for them to be in when you close them!

If you see another salesperson appearing to have trouble, don't try to help. You don't know what has been said, and you may say the same thing that the other salesperson said. If it didn't work the first time, the second time it usually drives the customer out of the store. One time a sales person was having trouble with a customer because the chairs didn't clear the pedestal legs. I walked by and heard this. I then suggested chairs that did clear the leg. The customer sighed and said yes, he knew about those, but he didn't like the style of them. He then left. The salesperson told me that he too knew about these chairs and had gone through the same thing with the customer. Only the second time was enough for the customer to give up hope.

If for any reason you need to turn your customers over to another salesperson this is how you do it. Always make the other salesperson seem better than you. They have been here the longest and know the most or something like that. Then explain to the other salesperson what the customers are looking for while the customers are there. This accomplishes two things, bad feelings by the customer for being passed off are avoided, (because now they're dealing with someone better) and it avoids the other salesperson having to question the customers all over again about what they want.

You cannot be prejudiced toward your customers. Very poor looking people can be very rich. Very rich looking people can be very poor. The only thing you can do is treat everyone as a human being. Some people dress poorly just to see how the salesperson treats them. The ones that ignore them or steer them to the bargain basement items they'd rather not deal with anyway. If after this kind of treatment at other stores you and your store treat them well, they will want to do everything they can to buy from you. This of course is true with rich or poor customers.

I've had many customers tell me that they appreciated not being treated condescendingly by me, like they were a lot of other places. They knew they didn't look rich, but that still did not mean they weren't going to buy. And then you have people who normally don't have money but for some reason, an insurance settlement, inheritance, etc. they now do. They don't usually change their poor appearance or their ways, but now they have money. I've sold many people like that. If you're the only one that treats them with respect, you have a customer for life. Anytime they do have money, they buy from you and you only. They know you treated them as the person they are, and they have a lot of bad experiences with other salespeople to compare you with.

However, customers can and are prejudiced about you. Realize this when you set your appearance. Sometimes customers are downright unfriendly with one salesperson and delightful with another. You never know the reason for this. Maybe you look like someone they had a bad experience with. Maybe it's your accent. Usually you will never know. If this happens to you and your customers seem to prefer another salesperson, let the other salesperson take them and you take another one. Why not? You probably can't sell them anyway, especially if they don't like you or don't feel at ease with you.

Accept the fact that some customers sexually stereotype. I would be asked over by a saleswoman to explain to a customer some question he had about the construction. The customer would thank me for taking time to explain it to him, and he would buy it. The saleswoman would say to me after they left that she had already told him the exact same thing before I got there, but he wouldn't take her seriously. I had the same problem when I would tell a woman what colors I thought went together. I would get no response, so I would ask a saleswoman her opinion. She would say the same thing I did, and the customer would act like it was the first time she'd heard that, and she would get it.

Men are supposed to know construction better than women do. Women are supposed to know styles and colors better than men. So when this sexual stereotyping happens to you, don't fight it. Deal with it and make the sale. That's the purpose you're there for. It's not to raise a customer's consciousness! You're not going to be able to do it anyway. Just sell and deal with people as they are, not as you would like them to be!

The main thing is to be open minded and to honestly observe people and their reactions to certain situations. Don't worry about your pride or ego. If you do something that doesn't have the desired effect, don't make believe it does. Change it so it works. Listen to other people's advice and try it. If it works, that's great. If it doesn't, keep trying something new.

Your purpose is to sell as many people as you can. Give each sale your best effort, no matter how much money is involved. Don't think about how much money you'll make on the sale while your selling.

Selling demands full attention. If you keep making sales, the money will follow. If your mind is cluttered with anything but selling, you won't do as well as you could.

Practice your presentations, know the steps and do them in order, but when the time comes to deal with customers, be relaxed, happy and just try to help them buy what they want. Don't worry about anything else. It makes for a nice vacation from whatever troubles you may be having!

Chapter Eighteen

How to Avoid Sales Slumps

Usually when someone first comes out of training, they sell just about everyone they talk to. There are two main reasons for this. One is that they only know the steps and the presentations and how to be themselves, so they do everything right. They know no other way. The other reason is they haven't got any prejudices about customers. They don't know certain types of people are harder to sell than others. So they give everyone their best shot. They go along great for a while and then their sales start taking a downward trend. They go into a slump.

What counts is what you did today, not yesterday. Slumps can be avoided if you know what causes them. I used to have them all the time. My used car salesman friend, Bill, never had them. I asked him how he did it. He put a wife and four children through college, plus bought a house in an expensive neighborhood selling used cars. He was a professional. He said if it works, don't fix it. If what you're doing is making sales, keep doing it.

What happens is that after giving the same presentation for the two thousandth time, salespeople start to get bored with it. So they start to vary it for their own sake. The other thing people would do is to do everything right in the beginning and do well. Then they start to think this is not that hard. They start to relax the process. They skip things they used to do and add other things they didn't.

Gradually their sales start to decline. They don't notice much difference at first. Then they start drifting more and more from the presentation. When it finally gets bad enough to notice, they start trying real hard. Then it's a Catch 22 situation. The harder they try, the worse they do. It's like anything else. When you try too hard you get tense. The other person senses this, and the natural reaction is to get away from tense people. Then they hit rock bottom. They can't sell anyone. Finally their manager or friend tells them that they're not following the steps at all.

The best way out of a slump is to start comparing what you're doing now with what you did when you were successful. You realize you're not doing the same thing. This is better than trying to figure out what you're doing wrong. Remembering what you did when things went well will put you back on track. You'll get back to the basics, the fundamentals. The key is follow the six steps, relax, and be yourself. That's all you have to do.

The way you can keep from getting into slumps is to just keep doing what works. Remember when you give the presentation that this is the first time the customer has heard it. It's like being in a long running play. The way you can keep giving the same lines day after day is that you have that live feedback from the customer or audience. They react the exact same way to the same lines over and over again. It amazes me that twenty years later, people still say, "Oh, wow", every time I tell them the legs are adjustable. Their enthusiasm about what you're saying is contagious. Continue to feed off it.

So the key is if it ain't broke don't fix it. Stay conscious of what you're doing. Don't stray from it. The gratitude and enthusiasm you get from the customer makes it all worth it. Not to mention the sales!

Well now you have a good idea of how to make a retail sale. Just follow the steps, stay in the moment, relax and be yourself. You'll do fine. Good Luck!